BURDEN

**Every Woman's Daily Guide to a
Healthy, Happy Life**

MICHELE HOWE

**Burden Lifters: Every Woman's Daily Guide
to a Healthy, Happy Life**

Copyright © 2013 by **Michele Howe**

Published by Patheos Press, a division of Bondfire
Books, Englewood and Colorado Springs, Colorado.

Cover art to the electronic edition copyright © 2013
by Bondfire Books, LLC.

See full line of Patheos Press titles at
www.patheos.com/Books/Patheos-Press.

See full line of Bondfire Books titles at
www.bondfirebooks.com.

Electronic edition published 2013 by Bondfire Books
LLC, Colorado. ISBN 9781629214702

Praise for *Burden Lifters*

Who doesn't have burdens they want lifted? Nobody I know. That's why Michele Howe's *Burden Lifters* comes at just the right time for me (and for you). Take a moment each day to read how God's amazing promise to "lift every burden" can be made real to you. Find out how, day-by-day, burdens can be cast away.

Hope Egan
Founder, BiblicalEatingResources.com
Author of *What the Bible Says about Healthy Living Cookbook.*

Who among us doesn't have burdens to bear? In her new book *Burden Lifters*, Michele Howe demonstrates through heartwarming personal examples how life's little and not-so-little burdens are the stuff of life—the stuff that helps us grow in spirit, mind, and body. For each burden, Michele gives us a call to action that empowers us with Holy Power so we can serve others with dignity and grace. You've done it again, Michele. Thank you for being so real!

Jory Fisher, J.D.
Coach, Mentor, Speaker
www.JoryFisher.com

If you are looking for personal encouragement or if you long to help others who hurt, read *Burden Lifters*. Michele Howe has given us a book that reads like a devotional about every area of need in a woman's life, but it also provides resources that propel the reader in the direction of positive, focused action steps. I love this book!

Carol Kent
Author of *When I Lay My Isaac Down*

Encouragement. I love the word. It comes from the core word *courage*. And that is exactly what *Burden Lifters* will bring to your soul. Howe writes though the eyes of grace to the weary and fainthearted. Her words are deeply moving and more than informational—her words are transformational. She teaches us what fearless living looks like—a life that is a little more courageous, kinder, and braver.

Tammy Hanson Maltby
Author of *The God Who Sees You*

Life on earth is woven with a tapestry of joy and hardships. In her newest book, Michele Howe shares some raw personal experiences to confirm she knows what hardship feels like. There are relatable stories about anything you've had to endure, from financial issues to parenting to health problems and much more. Additionally, she walks us through the weighted journey, guiding us to the "light" side, where Jesus lifts each burden. Engaging, helpful and uplifting.

Diane Markins
Author and Host of "Bold Living" radio show

Michele Howe has written a thought-provoking and powerful book. Michele manages to convey the age-old message of hope, trust and faith in the midst of burdensome storms through an engaging and optimistic style of writing that leaves the reader feeling uplifted and hopeful. Each chapter shares a 'lift my burden prayer' that is comforting and helps the reader express those hidden feelings embedded deep in our hearts. *Burden Lifters* is a book of unmeasurable love, courage and faith in the center of life's challenges. Michele Howe's book is a treasure and a must-read for anyone who has dealt with the tumultuous burdens of life.

Lynnis Woods-Mullins
Host of "The Wellness Journey—LIVE!" talk show

Honest and intimate, Michele Howe shares personal snapshots depicting the wrangling of weighty trials that deepen hope, build character, exercise endurance, grow compassion and hone community. She succinctly exemplifies how burdens confronted, experienced, and traversed surprisingly lead to healthier, happier lives.

Rhonda Owens
Freelance writer and contributor to
TheBetterMom.com

Burden Lifters encouraged me, challenged me, and comforted me as I read Michele Howe's wise and often vulnerable words. I highly recommend spending 30 days with this book as your companion and allowing God, through Michele's daily encouragements, to lift a few of your burdens.

Ginny L. Yttrup
Award-winning author of *Words*

I loved *Burden Lifters*! Michele Howe writes with the kind of easy, authentic style that makes you feel like you're having an intimate conversation with a good friend. She's written a beautiful book that somehow manages to load you up with wisdom, yet leave you feeling lighter. I highly recommend this book to anyone who feels weighed down by life or wants to better understand how to help relieve the burdens of others.

Heather Kopp
Blogger at HeatherKopp.com and author
of Sober Mercies.

Dedication

Children lighten labors.
Anonymous

To my darling "Grands"—
Logan and Tyler

Becoming a grandma has surpassed
my grandest expectations.
(As I suspect it always will.)

Table of Contents

Introduction

A few years back I ran across a quotation that made me smile whenever I spotted it. It ran like this, "Children lighten labors." Do they? The honest answer is sometimes yes, sometimes no. Child-rearing is a lot like most things in life. We have moments when our cups of love are overflowing and we couldn't imagine anything grander than loving on our darling little ones. Then we have those other moments . . . sometimes hours, days, weeks even, when we wonder why we were so eager to bring children into the world, let alone take the responsibility for raising them.

When I first read this quotation, I wasn't thinking about my own now adult children. Rather, I was dreamily relishing spending precious time with my one and only grandson, Logan. I thought a lot about him. What he looked like, how he smelled baby bath fresh, what his soft skin felt like, and how cuddly he was when I held him against my heart. The truth is, he lifted the burdens right from my heart.

Immediately prior to my grandson's birth, I had just undergone yet another shoulder surgery, and I was trying to recover as quickly as possible so that I was physically strong enough to hold my oldest daughter's first child. Some days, I felt confident I would be ready to be the kind of mom and grandma that my daughter and her family needed. Other days, I felt overwhelmed by how quickly the days were flying past, and my daughter's due date loomed large on my calendar while I still felt physically weak and severely limited in what I was able to accomplish. All I knew was that I had a picture in my mind of what I needed to be, and I was a far cry from that inner ideal snapshot. The burden felt so heavy. But God had something in mind he wanted me to teach about trusting in my own strength rather than looking to him for what I needed and submitting to his plan for me.

Like so many areas of life, we have this idea of what's expected of us, of what we need to do (or be), and reality simply doesn't match up. We end up feeling discouraged, overwhelmed, depressed, and frequently want to give up. The burdens seem to outweigh all the good glimmering in the background just outside our range of vision. If only we knew how to bypass the difficulties and see straight through to the blessings beyond the burdens.

During those early weeks of recovery and well into my grandson's first months, I learned to take stock of what really matters in this life. His new life with all its possibilities and promise became daily reminders of God's promise to make all things new, even for me with all my physical limitations. Each day, no matter how challenging it might be, is a good day. God's Word tells us that in Psalm 118:24, "This is the day the Lord has made; let us rejoice and be glad in it." It also reminds us to rejoice simply because he made it, not because it's a good day according to our standards or by our definition. God made it, so it's good (and there's good to be found in it.)

I've found that all my burdens can be lifted if my perspective is first to honor God by trusting him with whatever comes my way. That "whatever" often means physical pain that never ends, lots of sleepless nights, and an emotional weariness from fighting this battle day in and day out. And still, there are reminders new every morning that God can lift me above my circumstances and hold me secure in his love. See the pattern here?

First we honor God by trusting him with everything, and I mean *every little thing*. Next, we thank him for everything, and I mean *every little thing*, knowing that beyond the burdensome pain is blessing enough to make up for any and all our losses. Finally, we train our minds to see our challenges through the heavenly perspective that God will indeed uphold us, strengthen us, guide us, and bestow grace and love upon us each and every day, for his glory and our good.

Burdens. We all have them. The question is, what do we do with them? As we explore all kinds of weighty trials in the stories that follow, let's keep reminding ourselves (and each other) of Jesus' words in Matthew 11: 28–30, "Come to me, all you who are weary and burdened, and I will give you rest. Take my yoke upon you and learn from me, for I am gentle and humble in heart, and you will find rest for your souls. For my yoke is easy and my burden is light." Sounds like a dream promise to me, one I want to grasp hold of and never let go no matter what.

I believe Jesus wants us to come close, so that he can teach us how to live in this agonizingly broken world and do it well. He wants to lift our burdens because he loves us, and he wants to remind us just how much he loves us by offering lovely reminders along the way. He hasn't forgotten about us and he knows what we're facing before we even lift our heads from the pillow each morning. Jesus also knows just how to transform our heaviest burdens into beautiful blessings.

Why not begin asking him for his perspective on our problems today? As we throw the weight of our burdens onto his capable shoulders our lives will change in ways we cannot begin to imagine. I'm ready to cast off my burdens for good. How about you? Better still, how about we do it together?

Chapter One
Waiting: When Inner Calm Trumps Control

Wait for the Lord; be strong and take heart
and wait for the Lord.

—Psalm 27: 14

How do we get to the morning, to the
sunshine, to the joy? There is only one way.
By waiting for it.

—Ken Gire

I hate waiting. Like everyone else, I struggle against the ticking of the clock when I feel such a sense of urgency inside for something to change or for relief to come *right this minute* that I can scarcely breathe. By far, the longest wait I've ever experienced came the night I thought my daughter was dead. I remember sitting in the dark kitchen at 1:00 a.m. staring out the window into more blackness and pleading with God to bring her home. Was I sure he would? Not really.

At that period of her life, my daughter was partying and clubbing and putting herself into one dangerous situation (and relationship) after another. So smack in the middle of that tortuously sleepless night as I waited for her to call or to respond to my text message—for any sign of life from her—I wondered if *I* would make it through the night.

Somehow God reached into my heart and gave me just enough strength to keep breathing (and praying) as I waited, but it was the longest, most painful wait I've ever endured. This in part because I was keenly aware that there was nothing I could do but wait. In those terrifyingly dark hours, I honestly didn't know how God would answer my prayers. I didn't know if I'd ever see my beautiful daughter again. But I did know one thing for certain—that God waited with me.

* * *

What have you waited for? All of us have had experiences of desperate waiting, haven't we? We can all recall a few (or more) heart pounding, pulse-racing moments when God seemed absent but was really there right with us. Every one of us has experienced those times when we really believed we couldn't wait another moment for help or relief from a tragedy too large for us to handle. But what about those times when we're called to wait on the not so urgent? Those countless daily opportunities when it's not a life or death situation; it's purely uncomfortable and we simply don't like it?

We're a sorry bunch of "waiters" aren't we? Our entire nation wants, no, *demands* that needs be met immediately. Whether the coveted object(ive) is small or large matters not. Americans young and old are continually being fed the fabrication that if we desire something, it is within our power and rights to immediately obtain it. No delay required.

Real life begs to disagree. And disagree it does. Consider all that you've waited for in your own life. We wait to get better after feeling ill. We wait for someone to reply to an urgent request. We wait for doctors, dentists, hair stylists, spouses, children. We wait in lines. We wait for our turn. We wait to be heard. We wait to be found or found out. We wait for a better job. We wait to receive an education. We wait for repair technicians, for parts, for labor, for bills. We wait to hear the weather. We wait for the sports news, evening news, bad news, good news, and any news at all. Let's face it, for a huge portion of our lives we must wait.

Since, in large measure, waiting is life and life is waiting; why not learn to wait the best way we can? Let's switch around former assumptions and learn to view wait time as the opportune time to develop quietness, listen better, see more clearly, contemplate tough decisions, reflect, and be thankful. We can do this. We can. If we choose to use all that anxiety-ridden energy and channel it into a different direction, our waiting will be transformed.

If we can accept waiting as a necessary ally rather than a mortal adversary, everything about us will alter too. There will suddenly be more time for what's important, for appreciating the subtle beauty of daily life, and for resting contentedly wherever we find ourselves. We can take comfort that time is fluid, moving, and never stagnant. No matter how long the wait, or how painful, it won't last forever. History proves this. It should also convince us that there are moments and spaces of time when it is only after we traverse through the waiting stage that genuine hope arrives on the scene.

Author Ken Gire writes, "We can't hurry the dawn, no matter how anxiously we pace the floor or how impatiently we watch the clock. And so the question is not do we wait or not wait, because waiting is all we can do. The question is; how will we wait? Will we wait well . . . or will we wait poorly?"

Takeaway Thought: When we have no choice but to wait, God give me the strength to wait well and to wait upon you alone.

I lift my burden to you Lord,

Today and every day I am placed in a position where I must wait. Some days I wait well, but most days I struggle deeply to maintain a heart that is quiet and calm. Instead, I wrestle and fight against situations, people, and even parts of myself that I cannot control. Help me, Jesus, to still my heart and mind and to rest in you despite the outward circumstances that feel so unsettling, so threatening to me. Fill me with your wisdom, your understanding, and an awareness of your nearness to me always. Amen.

Chapter Two
Uncertainty: Risking Discomfort for the Sake of Another

God is our refuge and strength, an ever-present help in trouble. Therefore we will not fear, though the earth give way and the mountains fall into the heart of the sea.

—Psalm 46: 1–2

Some persons do first, think afterward, and then repent forever.

—Thomas Secker

I was afraid. I sat in the circle of women and listened to another woman talk about the difficulties in her marriage, and I could hear in her voice that she'd given up hope. I could see through her tears that she was risking a lot being so honest in a group such as ours. Everyone could see how desperate she felt, surely that's what compelled her to take the chance in being so brutally honest, risking judgment or pity or worse . . . silence. And at first, that's just what she got. Silence. No one said a word. Not a single word. And it was deafening.

I sat within four feet of this brokenhearted woman, but I could have been miles away for all the good I did her. Then I looked into her eyes, really looked at her, and my heart broke right along with hers. My heart started pounding, and I knew with all my heart that God wanted me to risk something right then and there. He wanted me to tell her she wasn't alone. God was prompting me to be honest too. He was urging me to reach toward this woman with the truth that I wasn't merely "with her" in the same room; I was in the same exact place in my own marriage. Hopeless. Hurt. Defeated. Beaten down. Torn apart.

I would like to say that I had great courage (or at least great eloquence) when I finally spoke up, but the truth isn't so glamorous (or impressive). All I recall saying was, "You're not alone in this, I understand. I'm feeling exactly the same way right now." Others in the room might well say the only helpful remark I made that day, after confessing how much I was hurting, was the Bible verse and principle I shared with her. But, if I'm really honest, I believe the most important thing I did was simply share the truth. If you saw the look her in eyes after I did, I'm sure you would agree.

* * *

How would you describe yourself? Are you a careful person, one given to thoughtfully weighing decisions and their repercussions before acting? Or would you consider yourself the free-flying, live-by-the-moment, carefree (careless) type? There is no right or wrong answer here. It's simply a matter of degree. Certainly, the individual who notices things—

you know, is in tune to the feelings, bents, and likes/dislikes of those around him—will act in accordance with what he observes. If he's careful, that is. There's nothing more boorish than a person who purposefully decides to offend, right?

On the flip side, there are those who appear to live within a world of their own making. It's those people who do what they please whenever, wherever, and to whomever they choose. Ick. All of us have been victim to someone's careless, self-serving decisions. We recognize the harm in it and so does everyone else, except maybe the offender.

But is there such a thing as living too carefully, too contemplatively? Indeed there is. Too much thinking, over-thinking, leads to fearful pausing, inaction, and lack of involvement. So to strike a balance between the two extremes, might we not aim for some middle road? Live with awareness that every choice made in favor of something is also a choice against something else. Given only so much time, energy, and resources, each of us decides how to best live, work, and play.

This fact leads to the next logical conclusion. Every decision we make today will support, strengthen, or contribute to the building up of people surrounding us—or it will tear them down. Which will it be? If we're given to living carefully, our lives will be full of strong relationships, better physical health, sounder finances, and overall increased bountiful living. Final word: Take good care. It is the recipe for a life of fullness.

Takeaway Thought: Most often, when I'm feeling afraid to step forward to help someone else, it's exactly the step I need to take.

I lift my burden to You, Lord,

Help me to never, ever waiver in stepping forward when I see someone in need. Whether I can offer help by word or deed, help me, Lord, to always do the right thing. Give me the strength I require to risk being hurt or rejected or ridiculed in order to lighten someone's burden. I know I do not have within me what it takes to heal a broken heart or mend a hopeless life, but I do know I can help, even a little, to ease another's pain. One choice, one opportunity at a time, help me, Lord, to step forward. Amen.

Chapter Three
Discouragement: Identifying the Blessing Amidst the Bruising

Why are you downcast, O my soul? Why so disturbed within me? Put your hope in God, for I will yet praise him, my Savior and my God.

—Psalm 42: 5–6

A season of suffering is a small price to pay for a clear view of God.

—Max Lucado

It's that time of year again. The particular season of the year when I'm prone to remembering some very specific difficult events and even more painful emotions. It used to be that fall was my favorite time of the year. But that was before my daughter's close friend was killed in an auto accident mid-October. And before my father in law died of esophageal cancer in early September. Memories are funny things, and sometimes I really believe they have a life of their own because without warning every fall, I find myself fighting the blues. Sadness comes out of nowhere and takes on colorfully surprising shapes in the same way the leaves on our trees suddenly turn into their own riot of color from one day to the next.

I'm not complaining about remembering, just contemplating how powerful our thoughts and recollections. If we don't take hold of them, they will surely take hold of us. I also know that the older we get, the more tough seasons we will have weathered, which in turn, creates more memories. Some good. Some not so much. As I pause for a few minutes and simply sit with my eyes closed and my heart wide open, I ask God for his perspective on my turbulent feelings. I've lived long enough to know this much: until I surrender my past, my present, and my future (memories and all) to his good will, I simply can't move past the pain of the past. Even the best of times will sour if I cling to them too tightly. So right now, I place myself at his disposal and ask for grace to remember what needs remembering and grace to put aside what I should forget.

* * *

Discouragement can come upon us without warning. When it does, we're often left wondering where on earth these dismal thoughts and feelings came from. Then we start remembering, and how we choose to dredge up the past makes a huge difference in today's days and hours. God's Word has much to say about the epidemic of discouragement that springs from a heart that fails to remember well.

The Israelites, who should have known better after God miraculously delivered them from the clutches of the king of Egypt and his army, didn't walk very far from their enemy's grasp before they started getting discouraged. They whined. They moaned. They groaned. God had mercy on them time after time, but he also gave them some advice: "Remember. Call to mind each and every act of love and faithfulness and provision that I've provided."

Remembering. It matters. Remembering *well* matters equally as much. Some of our recollections can skew us toward harboring resentment, bitterness, even hatred. Other memories might simply provoke feelings of sadness or regret. Let's not discount the power of our minds to recall both the good and bad that will influence us in significant ways today (for good or bad.)

Instead of focusing on and nurturing painful memories, let us choose to recall the good (even amidst the hard.) For we are told that all things most certainly do work together for good for those who are called according to his purpose. God, our great redeemer, can and does transform even the most heart-stopping, heart-breaking season of sorrow into something blessed and, eventually, beautiful. Transforming our thoughts is how we learn to identify the obstacles in our hearts and minds and to implement solutions by remembering well that our God is a loving God. And that's something he wants us to never forget.

Takeaway Thought: During the darkest seasons of life, God is building a history of faithfulness between himself and me that can never be shaken.

I lift my burden to you, Lord,

I freely admit that I am not good at remembering. All too often, I focus my thoughts on the pain of some past event or season instead of on how faithfully you met my needs at every step of the journey. Help me, Lord, to remember all things with a spirit of gratitude and thanks. Let me never forget that you are the promise keeper who loves and sustains me through all of life's seasons. Amen.

Chapter Four
Loss: Letting Go of That Which Holds Me Captive

How long, O Lord? Will you forget me
forever? How long will you hide your face
from me? How long must I wrestle with my
thoughts and every day have sorrow in my
heart?

—Psalm 13: 1–2

Life comes to women in stiff doses. When it
does, and we are crushed or shattered or
stretched beyond our limits, we need to
surround ourselves with good theologians.
But at the end of the day, it won't be their
theology we will lean on . . . . We will lean on
our own.

—Carolyn Custis James

This week was full of losses. Material losses. Political
losses. Health losses. Relational losses. Each and every
one made my heart and mind ache for relief. I felt like
yelling, "I give!" to God so that he'd put a stop to the
pain (and the losses). I so wanted to do a rewind and
replay for a different outcome in each of these areas.
But as much as I desired different, more favorable
results, I realized something.

As much as these losses stung, there was something deeper amiss in my heart. A single word: idols. From the loss of the election to some financial slippage to a recent relational tangle that made me feel heartsick (and body sick), I realized that in every single one of these situations I had made an idol out of getting the results I wanted (craved?). Idols. As one theologian said, our hearts are idol factories. We manufacture one after another throughout our lives. Each time we do, they come crumbling down, and we look at the mess in grave disappointment because we were so hoping they'd come through for us in a much deeper level than they were ever intended.

Desiring what I believed to be right and true and honorable resulted in my losses, but I also had to admit that it wasn't just the multiplication of loss that was getting to me. It was the accompanying disappointment. In life. In myself. In God. I have to continually remind myself that life and losses go hand in hand throughout this broken world. No amount of hoping, wishing, or praying otherwise is going to change the fact that we all live in a dying world. But once we accept that truth, our losses make more sense and don't take us by surprise so much. Loss upon loss, we need to walk hand in hand with God through it all. And yes, it's still going to hurt and sting like crazy.

* * *

Losses come to us all. Sometimes those losses are our own fault. Other times we experience loss at the hands of others. Often, losses come by no fault of any person, it's simply part and parcel of this damaged, sin-ridden world. But when the losses come, we have to be prepared. Each of us has to know what we believe before the storms hit. Otherwise, we'll tumble and fall deeper and faster and farther than if we'd been prepared on the inside of our hearts and minds.

How does one prepare for the inevitable without sounding like a naysayer? By becoming a student of the Bible and rightly understanding what God's Word says about life on this planet. Scripture clearly teaches that we will have trouble but that we shouldn't let it overcome us. Why? Because Jesus overcame the world. That's the good news. The bad news is that we're going to experience trouble, pain, and loss upon loss.

Once we come to accept that struggle is part of life, every life, then we're much more ready to respond to life's difficulties and disappointments with a grace-laced answer. What does a grace-laced answer look like? One that speaks the promises of God's provision out loud, by faith, and keeps on speaking out the truth that God said he would provide. Period. It's true, we often don't understand why these losses come to us, but we can bank on a single truth found in God's Word through them all. Those who trust in the Lord will not be disappointed. He said it, we need to believe it before, during, and after our losses.

Takeaway Thought: My losses are God's best opportunities to set me free from the inside out.

I lift my burden to you, Lord,

Help me to see this world with all its pain, suffering and loss through the lens of eternity. I need your perspective when I hurt so deeply, Lord. Sometimes the constant barrage of bad news overwhelms me to the point where I want to give up. Losing something or someone I love just plain hurts. Give me the wisdom and grace and the strength I need to keep placing my heart, broken and all, into your faithful hands. Amen.

Chapter Five
Depression: When Changes Lift Emotions

I wait for the Lord, my soul waits, and in his word I put my hope.

—Psalm 130:5

Depression is an occasion for re-evaluating and changing.

—Edward T. Welch

Although it has been years since I experienced a season of deep depression (over eight years to be exact), I remember so much about that dismal summer. It felt like a tsunami hit me of out nowhere. Like many folks, I knew men and women who struggled with depression, and I felt sorry for them, commiserated with them, and wanted to ease their pain. The truth is, once I became depressed myself, I finally recognized this was one area in life that unless you've gone through the muck and mire of it, you simply cannot fully understand the depth of depression's pain. Nor can you navigate a quick way out.

Two specific memories are etched in my mind's eye even today of that difficult summer. It happened when my body was recovering from the first of now six shoulder surgeries, when I was lying awake night after night exhausted but sleepless, after our family had just ended a long period of care-giving for an elderly relative, and once we'd made the heart-wrenching decision to leave our church home of over twenty-two years. Knowing what I know now, I should have seen depression approaching. I didn't. But I'll never forget the lessons God had for me in that dark place.

As clear as day, I remember sitting alone on the grass in the midday sun hunched over my Bible and realizing that since my emotions had gone AWOL, I would have to take God's Word, well, at his word. Promises that had in the past made me feel better, more hopeful, encouraged, and energized, held nothing for me now. I honestly couldn't feel anything but an eerie complacent deadness. And it was utterly frightening.

But I could cry, could I ever cry. Which led me to my second vivid recollection when I made an urgent cry-for-help phone call to my best friend. With tears streaming down my face and a catch in my voice, I cried out for help. She listened carefully, silently until I was cried out. Then she spoke. Simply and with resolve, my friend's words were, "I know you don't believe this is ever going to end, but it will. I know you don't believe (in God's faithfulness or your own strength to get through), but I'm going to believe with you and for you until you can believe on your own again." Those precious, simply stated words were the starting point of my overcoming my depressed state. At that moment, I didn't feel any better, but at that moment I became determined to get better. And I did.

* * *

Depression remains one of the most common yet elusive conditions to understand. Some believe it's a physiological problem alone. Others, an emotional one. For Christians, many believe it's a spiritual malady that can be cured by words of confession and self-flagellating acts of denial. For me, I believe it's a combination of our choices and experiences, which in turn, lead to physical, emotional, mental, and spiritual repercussions.

As physical beings, no one can discount the stress our bodies endure day in and day out, which can frequently burn us out. Thus, depression can be triggered by misusing or over-using our bodies, even in the pursuit of worthy goals. Emotions, too, can grow so taut with intense and demanding constant use that they finally give way to the depressed state of an "I give up" mentality. Spiritually speaking, Scripture is clear that when we choose anger, bitterness, resentfulness, and revenge; that brittleness of the bones, weakness of muscles, and sleeplessness are close companions.

Depression finds its birthplace in countless ways and can put a stranglehold on a heart and life before a person realizes what has happened. Which is why each of us needs to take time to evaluate and re-evaluate the ways in which we govern our lives. From the daily physical care of our bodies to how we work through life's disappointments and pain, it all matters. Our choices and how we choose to think about life's challenges can either press us down further into deep depression or lift us up out of it.

Moment by moment, hour by hour, day by day we make choices. Those decisions we make, in turn, make us. I've always loved the put-off, put-on mentality of biblical living. With intention we put off disbelief, unforgiveness, anger, and the like while intentionally putting on belief, forgiveness, hope, and every other life-giving, uplifting thought and action.

Honestly evaluating ourselves and our lives takes courage. But without periodic (even frequent) self-checks, it is all too easy to find ourselves spiraling downward like powerless victims rather than able-bodied, strong-minded, faith-filled individuals who look at the future with a glad heart and a spirit of optimism.

Takeaway Thought: I count on God's never-changing goodness and faithfulness, which is so much more trustworthy than any of my ever-changing feelings and emotions.

I lift my burden to you, Lord,

Today you know the pain I'm feeling emotionally, Lord. Will you help by lifting my thoughts to you? Enable me to focus my energies on who you have promised to be for me. Even though I cannot feel happy at this moment, help me to harness my thoughts and recognize all I have to be thankful for, and then speak out words of gratitude to you. By faith, Lord, I trust you to see me through this season. Amen.

Chapter Six
Exhaustion: Rest for What Wearies Me

Find rest, O my soul, in God alone; my hope
comes from him.

—Psalm 62: 5

One of life's little ironies is that some of our
hardest times are when our dreams actually
do come true.

—Paula Rinehart

Nothing compares to a sleepless night. Unless, of
course, you string together a whole bunch of sleepless
nights in a row, then you experience not only physical
exhaustion but a special brand of craziness too. I've
been there in the not so distant past, and my memory
of those months when I couldn't sleep about drove
me crazy.

Looking back, it was the perfect storm of events
that took me to my knees hour by hour in complete
and overwhelming exhaustion. If it wasn't one (or
both) of my loose shoulders paining me through
those dim hours, it was the continual onslaught of hot
flashes that stirred me out of sleep with a sudden and
violent pounding in my heart that momentarily
preceded an inside-out drenching. Hour after hour, I
would wake up and have a difficult time going back

to sleep. After a few months of this nonsense, I began hating bedtime. This is saying a lot since one of my favorite comforts in life has been a good night's sleep.

I tried everything I could find to counteract the combination of pain and hot flashes. Nothing worked. I cried out to God to please send me someone or something to help me because I was out of solutions and feeling more desperate as the days went by. In the midst of my delirium I learned to never, ever take God's promised provision for granted. It just didn't come packaged as I had hoped.

I also learned to never say never when no amount of exercise, eating plans, vitamin regimes, or holistic solutions worked. After all my effort, I was forced into a corner with few options left except pharmaceutical ones. My physician offered me a short stint on HRT (hormone replacement therapy) and, though kicking and screaming, I agreed to try it. Immediately, my quality of life increased one hundred fold. Sleeplessness was a thing of the past, but I was forced to accept the hard truth that when I ask for God's help, he has the prerogative in how to supply my need. Sometimes, I truly believe he allows us to get really uncomfortable so we can hear him better. And, so that we're reminded God is the creator, sustainer, and life-giver.

* * *

We all like to believe we're in control of our lives. We love to mentally tabulate that what we've achieved is all a result of our own doing. For sure, it's our blood, sweat, and tears that got us the job, house, spouse, friends, or vacation. As Americans, we've got the corner on independence. But it's not true.

Every single one of us is where we are in life because of God's good gifts of specific talents, bents, abilities, and blessings. If we're born with superior intelligence, thank God. If we're born with physical strength and stamina, thank God. If we're born into a family with parents who love us, thank God. Still, we often forget that who we are and what we accomplish is always sustained by our heavenly Father.

We like to believe that if we take good enough care of our bodies, our minds, our souls, then God will pave a smooth path in front of us. This isn't what Scripture teaches. In fact, over and over, Jesus tells us we will have trouble (lots of it) in this life. The good news is that Jesus has overcome this world and all its troubles. Once we accept that doing the right things into exhaustion won't inoculate us from the world's pain (physical, emotional, mental), then we can learn to rest from that which wearies us.

Throughout those tedious months of long, sleepless nights, I begged the Lord to allow me one good night's sleep. For months on end, that prayer went unanswered (from my human perspective). In the worst moments of my exhaustion—when it was hard to concentrate and speak a coherent sentence—I felt my humanity, my frailty, and my weakness more keenly than ever before. And I learned something during those dark hours when everyone else was slumbering sweetly; I realized how much I count on God for every breath I take. In and out, in and out, it's all him. It always was, I just hadn't realized that truth yet.

All our laboring is in vain. It is. He wants to give us rest. Regular daily (and nightly) rest to recharge and rejuvenate our bodies, our minds, our souls. It is one of life's ironies that often when we believe everything is going our way, we are in reality struggling more mightily than ever. The lesson I know to be true is this, God governs our days and nights, and whether we work or we sleep, he longs to give us rest from whatever wearies us. Our choice is to come into his quiet presence long enough to hear him speak.

Takeaway Thought: I can do a little or a lot, but none of my labor makes any difference if the Lord would rather have me resting instead.

I lift my burden to you, Lord,

I am perpetually exhausted. No matter how little or how much I plan to do each day, I end up feeling worn out. Lord, help me to take more time at the beginning of every new day to sit in stillness before you. I need your input, your guidance, and your direction. Otherwise, I wind up running in circles accomplishing much to my own mind but perhaps of little value to yours. Help me to gladly accept the good gift of daily rest you offer me because you love me. Amen.

Chapter Seven
Sorrow: When Love Triumphs over All

You keep track of all my sorrows. You have collected all my tears in your bottle. You have recorded each one in your book.

—Psalm 56:8

Sorrow can go only as deep as love. And always, always, love is the ground beneath sorrow as well as the sky above it.

—Gregory Floyd

Some years ago I received a phone call asking for prayer for a young couple whose baby girl had been born without eyes just hours earlier. I distinctly recall my knees buckling when I heard the news. This lovely couple had already faced down years of infertility problems and multiple miscarriages. Everyone who knew them was overjoyed when this mom's pregnancy went full term. This made the news of their baby girl's condition at her birth that much harder to bear. Sorrow shadowed my heart for days as I prayed for this dear family to sense God's gentle hand of care upon their daughter and to continue seeking him for what they would now be facing as parents of a special needs child.

Like so many other moms of physically healthy children, I considered how I would have reacted to this same devastating news seconds after having given birth. My dreams, my desires, and my hopes for that child would suddenly be dashed against the reality of a very different and uncertain future than the one I had nurtured for nine months. My heart ached at the thought. I felt sorrow for this family, and I wondered how they would get through these early days and weeks when the shock would be the most brutal to grasp and accept.

Slowly then, God began redirecting my thoughts along very different lines. He reminded me through verses I'd read over and over again through the years that he created this little girl perfectly (Psalm 139.) He wasn't sitting in heaven wringing his hands in surprise and despair over her condition. Rather, God was celebrating the birth of another life carefully planned and designed by him alone. A life that he would watch over, guard, protect, nurture, and rejoice in.

As that heavenly perspective started to take hold in my thoughts, God taught me once again that a good life by his standards often looks radically different from what man thinks is good. His way is always best, even when our hearts are breaking apart in sorrow— maybe especially then.

I've watched this little family add two more children to their numbers, and time and again, I've been blessed, encouraged, and challenged by how God transformed a seemingly tragic event into something utterly beautiful. So much so, you'd have to see it to believe it. All because of love that sees past what most folks see.

* * *

When we realize we've hurt someone, we say we're sorry. Hopefully, those aren't just superficial words to mend a rift in a relationship. If we're truly sorry for something, we feel regret and sorrow inside our hearts and minds. Yes, sorrow is the much deeper expression of simply feeling bad. Sorrow is that heart aching, sick-to-my-stomach feeling we get when we hear terrible news or when something truly tragic happens to someone we love. Sadly, sorrow is part of this world, and no one is immune from its pain.

With sorrow comes grief, sadness, and sometimes the death of a dream, a relationship, or even a life. One of the aspects of sorrow that we frequently miss is that feeling sorrowful means we care. It means love is at the foundation of that emotion. If we love someone, we will naturally feel sorrow for him or her when they hurt. Sorrow is the right response in the face of tragedy. It is the appropriate emotion to feel and then harness to help make the situation better.

Without sorrow, none of us would be moved to act for another. We would more resemble robots that process incoming data devoid of emotion. Instead, God gave us these emotions as part of his perfect design. He wants us to be moved by sorrow so that we step out and move toward others with help, hope, and healing. Sorrow—we may not like it, but we can't live without it.

Lest we doubt that sorrow is a good gift from our God, let's remind ourselves that Jesus, who is our example in all things, was a man for whom sorrow and grief were close companions.

Takeaway Thought: Your love, Lord, is what sustains us during life's most painful and painfully confusing moments. We may never understand the whys of life, but we willingly cling in trust to the who sovereignly ruling over it all.

I lift my burden to you, Lord,

Just when I get a handle on one piece of bad news, another comes along. It does feel like too much sorrow to bear. Even when the tragedy isn't affecting me personally, it still hurts me deep inside as I imagine the pain another is facing. Lord, help me to accept that it is not possible for my mind to comprehend the bigger story of my life here on earth. Help me to survive and thrive here by developing a robust faith and trust in you and then move forward to help others who are suffering. Amen.

Chapter Eight
Giving Up: Friends Who Remind Us Why It's Never Okay

You God stoop down to make me great. You broaden the path beneath me, so that my ankles do not turn.

—Psalm 18: 35–36

God never wastes pain. He always uses it to accomplish His purpose.

—Jerry Bridges

There's something about being in physical pain that makes me wary of taking on new projects, tiring volunteer opportunities, even fun leisure activities. I know this to be true. For years, I've been in almost constant pain, and though I've accepted the fact that my shoulder problems will continue to remind me of my untreatable condition both day and night, I have my days (did I mention nights?) when it gets to be too much.

When I wake up to the sound of rain hitting the rooftops, I can pretty much plan on having to fight extra hard not to be waylaid by pain that day. If I've traveled in a car for more than twenty minutes, picked up a heavy grocery bag, or gone on a cleaning tear through the house, I can expect to pay for it. And I do, for not one but usually several days thereafter.

My biggest battle isn't accepting that I have a physical condition that no amount of surgery, drugs, or exercise can cure, it's my tendency to project ahead that gets to me the most. With Christ's help, I can do today, painful as it might be. On my own though, I tend to look far into the future and quickly find myself sinking into despair. I wrongly allow my mind to wander into the months and years ahead and see myself still fighting this daily pain, and I want to give up.

On particularly difficult days when I have a to-do list a mile long and my pain level is ratcheting up and up and up, I've found only one sure-fire remedy: call a friend.

During those "I want to give up" moments, I need a fresh perspective, a good word of encouragement, or maybe just a laugh. Thankfully, I know where to turn. Friends. One and all have helped me see life better, brighter, and with a whole bunch of hope all wrapped up in love. I wonder about people who say they don't need friends, because I sure wouldn't want to live my life without them at my side.

* * *

One of the great things about female friendships is you don't always need a lot of words to convey a lot of meaning. In fact, sometimes just a look will do the job. (Or a single word text).

This is why I'm so grateful to have a small gang of my own to call friends.

Fall, winter, spring, or summer—it doesn't really matter what season we're in or what holiday we're celebrating because rejoicing in the friendships we share with others is always the "gift that keeps on giving." This is especially true for females.

Women and their friendships: Their solidarity is confounding, given they often agree and disagree in equal measure; yet their loyalty pronounces a unity that can't be disputed. Good friends won't let each other fall too far. They have each other's backs. They feel each other's pain. They sometimes feel like a pain, true enough. And still, when the losses tally up, women rally to one another's sides and secure the gap with a commitment so tenacious it can be startling to onlookers as well as the women themselves.

Friends reach out and secure one another. They reach under and lift up. They reach around and hold tight. Surrounded by such a safety net and secured by unconditional love, it's no wonder that women fare better than their male counterparts in the wake of similarly devastating circumstances. It's true, there is indeed safety in numbers; and the language of friendships can offer something precious, not to replace the loss mind you, but to circumvent some measure of the hurt. It is standing and declaring publicly, "This is my friend." Real friends make a woman feel safe, inside and out. Safe.

Secure. For sure.

Takeaway Thought: When I'm afraid that I don't have the strength to keep facing this battle, you use my dear friends to hold me up.

I lift my burden to you, Lord,

Thank you for the blessings of good and faithful friends you've given me, Lord. You know the times when I need someone else to listen to my fears and concerns and then point me back toward you. I never feel alone after I've shared my sinking heart with a good friend. And please, please Lord, help me to never get so caught up in my own pain that I neglect the hurts of others. Make me sensitive to the spoken and unspoken needs of my friends, and help me to do whatever it takes for them to know they are well loved. Amen.

Chapter Nine
Hopelessness: How Today's Challenges Fortify Me for Tomorrow

The Lord is my portion; therefore I will wait
for him. The Lord is good to those whose
hope is in him, to the one who seeks him.
                                    —Lamentations 3: 24-25

Sometimes following God means throwing
caution to the wind. Sometimes caution is a
symptom of faithlessness.
                                    —Carolyn Custis James

My friend's daughter was extremely sick. Whatever mystery illness was plaguing her was starting to shut down her organs. For years my good friend and her teenage daughter searched for a medical answer to this frighteningly debilitating condition. Doctor after doctor, specialist after specialist, hospital after hospital, these two women fought for answers as they simultaneously battled for the daughter's life.

This struggle endured for years. Not weeks. Not months. Years. The teen grew into a young adult woman before they found the medical help she needed and a long sought after diagnosis. Imagine that moment when someone finally got it right. They were thankful to God for answering thousands of tear-laced prayers that extended over countless seasons.

But with the diagnosis came a grim reminder of the damage already done by a delayed treatment plan—the virus had infiltrated every part of this young gal's body, and it would take vigilance and years to heal her. More treatments. More years. More tears. Enter the battle against hopelessness for the foreseeable future.

After expending much of the last decade of their lives and more money than they could afford to spend it was a bittersweet ending to a long battle. True, now they had a name for this insidious invader. They also had to face the fact that the fight wasn't nearly over. This mom and her daughter took risks others thought were silly, foolish even. But as desperate as they were, mother and daughter decided together to go the unconventional route with only God's inner assurance as their guide. Their faith-infused risk paid off.

Today, they're still entering a battle zone every single day but all they went through to get here has made them that much more resilient and hopeful. The truth is, we don't grow strong during the high times in life. We grow as we fight our way out of the thorny brambles and bushes with our bare hands. Sometimes our toughest battles are the stepping-stones that create an unbreakable foundation for a hope-infused life.

* * *

There's an old saying that says, "Whatever doesn't kill you will make you stronger," and I'd have to agree. There is something about being backed into a corner, facing down terrific foes that forces us to examine and then re-examine who we are and what we believe. In these scary moments, we had better already have figured out who and what we're going to put our trust in, because once the battle ensues, we won't have the time or the energy to be reflective.

Which is why everyone needs to spend some generous amounts of time reflecting on their belief system. I make my best effort to spend time daily with God, in his Word, praying, journaling, and reading thoughtfully challenging books by authors' way smarter and wiser than me. It makes all the difference in my day, all the difference between hopeless and hopeful.

My friend will tell you that what sustained her and her family during their most hopeless hours was the time she invested sitting alone before God and meditating upon the promises found in the Bible. She literally soaked up these comforting and powerful truths. Enough so that when it was time to move forward into foreign medical territory, she was equipped to do so from the inside out. My friend knew whom she believed and she counted him faithful to see her through. Come close to him today, before, during, and after you really need to do so. Come close. Recklessly close.

Takeaway Thought: Whatever I face today equips me for whatever I may face tomorrow.

I lift my burden to, you Lord,

No one likes to experience hopelessness, especially when it involves a situation where we have little control. In the midst of these desperate times, even my best effort gets me nowhere. And yet, there is a part of me that is comforted in the realization that you are in control, and it is your strength that will get me through. I admit it, when I feel most vulnerable I come running to you. Give me the wisdom to come running to you during those times when I don't feel needy or afraid. Give me the good sense to realize that being close to you is always the safest place to be. Amen.

Chapter Ten
Confinement: When Opting for Less Is Way More

Let us come before him with thanksgiving.
—Psalm 95: 10

Perhaps lifestyle disease is communicable.
You catch it through prosperity.
—Will Samson

Over the past eight months, I've been opening my mouth wide and staring at the ceiling in my dentist's office while enduring more dental work than I ever dreamed possible. All because of a kernel of popcorn gone awry that I inadvertently crunched down hard on some twenty-five years ago. That little decision to munch on those burnt kernels cost me. Over and over and over again.

The story goes like this; I bit down on the itsy-bitsy burnt kernel and felt a pain surge through my jaw. Unbeknownst to me, I had cracked a filling I'd had since I was a kid. My next dental checkup revealed the damaged filling needed replacing with a pricey gold crown. Some months later, I cracked the tooth under the said pricey crown and never felt it break. This led to a permanent bridge over three teeth. This bridge became part of me for over twenty-three years.

Last fall during a routine checkup, an x-ray revealed the bridge was loose, which meant it had to come off, which meant wrenching it off with some pretty mighty muscle power, which meant I shuddered every time I played that gruesome scenario over in my mind. Over the next few months, I went in, and in again, and yet again to have a tooth repaired, a root canal completed, a post inserted, and another permanent bridge made covering four of my teeth. Each time they tilted the chair back and told me to open wide, I regretted that one little decision to eat that kernel of popcorn. Who would have thought that I would still be paying for that inconsequential choice over a quarter of a century later?

Aside from the cost of this dental work, I paid in full (plus some) by feeling anxious, wary, and downright confined (physically, emotionally, and financially) during these procedures. I realized I was at the mercy of my dentist and his technician, because once the dental work begins there is no turning back. I also recognized I was at the mercy of our bank account, because our dental insurance didn't nearly touch the cost of this work.

To say I felt frustrated with myself would be an understatement. While this whole experience wasn't one of life and death proportions, it necessarily altered my life in little ways for months on end. As I sat in that dental chair, I gave a lot of thought as to how our choices confine us more than we realize.

One small decision can bring sudden and immediate consequences we hadn't anticipated. One tiny choice can domino into a hundred more weighty fall-outs. A single extravagant splurge can set us back for months on end. Like it or not, our choices either set us free or they confine and then confound us.

While I hope I never, ever, have to endure all those long hours in a dental chair again, I will say those hours when I had my mouth open (but couldn't say a word) gave me plenty of time to silently mull over the blessing of living with less and the freedom that comes along with that lifestyle.

* * *

How often do we consider our material prosperity as one of the main hindrances to our faith? Do we ever even think about the disparity of what we have, and consume, as citizens in the U.S. compared to the rest of the world? The fact is there have been a number of studies that show a direct correlation between increased material goods and inner dissatisfaction.

Amazing that we can gain more stuff by way of being over-zealous consumers and yet wind up unhappier than ever says a lot about the power of our choices and how our hearts affect our decisions. One choice, a single decision, over time, adds up to a lifetime of being confined by our stuff or set free by embracing an attitude of contentment.

Less is more. Always has been, always will be. Jesus talks about the dangers of loving money (or the stuff greenbacks can buy) more than loving him. In fact, the cautions against the pursuit of wealth are one of the most talked about subjects in the Bible. The lesson is simple. It's either a never-enough lust for more money, which breeds a life of confinement or a life of blessed, contented freedom. What will you choose?

Takeaway Thought: The choices I make today will either make me freer or serve to confine me further tomorrow.

I lift my burden to you, Lord,

These past months I've spent a great deal of time contemplating my life and asking myself the hard questions. When advertisers shout that I need what they have to sell, let me silence their voices with your truth. May I enjoy a contented peacefulness that can only arise from a heart that is focused and set on pleasing you, Lord. Please remove from my heart anything that distracts me from what matters most in this life. Everything I am, everything I have, is yours by rights. Always has been, always will be. Help me to steward well that which you've entrusted to me. Amen.

Chapter Eleven
Regret: When Mistakes Transform Us

When you (God) open your hand, they are
satisfied with good things

—Psalm 104:28

Candles seem to create peace. You don't find
candles lit in frenetic houses; you find them lit
in houses where people are trying to pay
attention.

—Lauren Winner

I should have listened to him. "Him" being my
husband. It felt like an "aha!" moment that arrived a
little too late for much damage control to take place.
And yet, isn't our God the one who promises to
restore the years the locusts have eaten? He sure is,
and I'm sure my family is thankful for that promise.

Many years ago I started writing books for single
moms, not because I've ever been a single parent, but
because two of my closest friends almost
simultaneously went through unwanted divorces of
their own. When they became single parents, I began
telling their stories. After watching my two friends
become both mom and dad to their children, nothing
seemed harder to me than parenting solo.

So why did I struggle so mightily against listening to my spouse's counsel regarding one of our children? To this day, I'm not quite sure. If I'm honest, I suppose I thought I had a better take on the situation because I was a woman overflowing with female emotions whereas my husband was all manly business. The truth is, I wasn't seeing the whole picture, and my inability (and unwillingness) to budge from my stance cost my daughter in a big way.

How does a mom spell regret? In big, bold, flashing neon letters that never stop blinking across this mother's mind, that's how. If only I had listened. If only I had trusted another's voice other than my own. If only I had taken more time to pray. If only I wasn't so impatient to fix a problem. My "if onlys" were adding up in part because I hadn't taken time to truly pay attention.

I didn't pay attention to what my spouse was observing. Pay attention to the signs that my daughter was making poor decisions. Pay attention to what the Lord was trying to tell me, that all my good intentions didn't amount to much (or avail much), if I wasn't hearing what he (the Lord) was trying to tell me. And more often than not, he (God) uses those closest to me to direct me—my husband, my kids, my parents, and my friends.

Paying attention takes effort. Listening takes effort. Waiting on the Lord takes effort (and self-control) to not rush headlong into a situation only to be left with regrets. Paying attention—it's a good thing.

* * *

Regret is the definitive thief. It robs us of our peace today. It steals our hope for tomorrow. Everyone has regrets. Be those regrets of the personal or professional variety, we all make mistakes and with our blunders come all sorts of repercussions.

It's true enough that when we have a fallout with someone, feelings are hurt and relational repair work has to be done. When we fail at work, again some repair duty must be had. But often we forget that there's another type of regret-worthy mistake we neglect to consider.

When we stop listening to the people in our lives who know us better than we know ourselves, there's trouble a brewing. When we fail to heed the advice of those who see the situation from every angle while we only see it from our side, there's going to be some heartache a happening. When we rush into a difficult situation without first stopping to pray and ask for God's wisdom, there's going to be some messy untangling to do.

It just makes sense. Before we leap into the fire (even when we have the best motives possible), we should take on the fireman's motto of stop, drop, and roll. Stop to get all the facts. Drop to our knees in prayer. Roll gently into the situation covered in gentleness and grace. If we can master those three steps, we can alleviate a good portion of the regret we'd experience otherwise. The best part of making mistakes? They can make us better people as we start paying attention to what we did wrong and then learn from it. And transforming something painful into something beautiful? That's a good thing too.

Takeaway Thought: When I rush into a situation as a fixer rather than patiently waiting on the Lord and heeding others' counsel, I generally make the problem worse.

I lift my burden to, you, Lord,

Far too often I run headlong into trouble in an attempt to make it all better or to make it all go away. Lord, I desperately need your perspective, your grace, your good word of instruction embedded deeply into my heart and mind. The more consistently I dig into your timeless truths, the more easily I am able to trust you with even the most heart-breaking situations that threaten to undo me emotionally. Help me to slow down and steadily, step-by-step, move into deeper trust in you alone. Amen.

Chapter Twelve
Disappointment: Harnessing Expectations to Fit Reality

In God they trusted and were not
disappointed.

—Psalm 22:5

When you taste a measure of being able to
love and enjoy the people in your life, without
having to have any particular response from
them, you are tasting bliss.

—Paula Rinehart

Sitting in a swivel chair completely covered by a gown, I sat with my eyes shut tight (but my ears wide open) as my lifelong friend (and almost as lifelong hair stylist) shared with me the tricks of her trade.

I had come into her salon with a weary heart and she knew it. We bounced around topics faster than she was putting color on my hair and snipping away all my split ends.

Knowing that she listens to countless men and women tell their stories and unburden themselves each and every day, I couldn't help but ask the question, "How do you hear so much bad news every day and not allow it to take you under emotionally? Don't you get overwhelmed at people specifically and at life in general by the end of the day?"

Believe me, I was all ears, because of late it seemed most of the news I had been hearing was painfully hard to take in, or take on, and I was feeling the weight of burdens not meant for me to carry. One person hurting another person. One individual betraying another. The stories, the heartbreaks, went on and on.

My friend sort of laughed and then told me her trick. After years of having taken on too many of her clients' problems, and carrying them home with her, she finally realized an important truth. She could be a caring listener and a messenger of encouragement, but she wasn't anyone's healer, or anyone's savior.

Bingo! As soon as she uttered the words, I felt like someone zinged me right in the heart with a truth I needed to grab hold of and never let go. I can be someone's listening ear. I can offer some words of counsel and advice. I can pray, and I do. But I am never, in any circumstance, someone's savior and messiah. No one is to take the place in another's life. Jesus. Savior. Messiah. Everything I say and do should point people to him, the only one who will never, ever disappoint.

* * *

Disappointment and expectations run hand in hand. The higher our expectations of people, places, and things, the harder these unrealistic hopes fall when they fail us. The only thing we can count on is that the more we expect a person, or any God-substitute, to take the place that God created just for him, we will suffer the same corresponding measure of emotional pain. The truth is, when I expect too much from you and you let me down, I'm going to really feel a down and out heartache. Perhaps unreasonably so, and that's my problem, not yours.

The more we harness our expectations and rein them in to fit with reality, the better off we are. The better off our relationships are. Any time we make another person our personal savior or messiah, we're in trouble, they're in trouble, and the relationship is in trouble. The more we look to God to meet our needs, the fitter we are to start forgetting about ourselves and begin looking out for the needs of others. It's a win-win scenario for us and for everyone we come into contact with.

If we place our main focus on God as the lover of our souls and as the provider of our every need, we are freed up to love and enjoy those in our lives more fully. When we learn to turn toward God to get our needs met, we in turn learn how to seek out and meet the needs of others. Our expectations then aren't unrealistic ones anymore, they are guided by the principle of doing unto others as we would have them do unto us. In other words, we start loving others with a generosity of spirit we never possessed before we gave up our unrealistic expectations that morphed into deeper disappointments with the person or the relationship.

Who wouldn't want to discover the path to loving others lavishly from the inside out? That's where the freedom lies. That's where the fun begins. Forgiveness. Fellowship. Freedom. Bliss. Pure Bliss.

Takeaway Thought: Instead of placing my trust in a person, place, or thing, I choose to place my whole trust in God alone who will never, ever disappoint me.

I lift my burden to you, Lord,

People, places, and things will eventually if not immediately disappoint me. Lord, you never will. Help me to appreciate and love the people in my life without expecting a higher standard of faultlessness than any human can ever attain. Give me your generosity of spirit and enable me to see people through the lens of your unconditional love. Always, always, lend me your eternal perspective and let my love for others be both deep and wide. Amen.

Chapter Thirteen
Broken Dreams: Piecing Together What Matters

The Lord is close to the brokenhearted and saves those crushed in spirit.

—Psalm 34: 18

Ours is not a culture that is comfortable with sadness. Sadness is awkward. It is unsettling. It ebbs and flows and takes its own shape. It beckons to be shared. It comes out in tears, and we don't quite know what to do with those.

—Nancy Guthrie

It was in the early spring when my daughter started training for the Chicago Marathon, her first ever marathon. I was watching her get up early to run "short runs" of six or seven miles a day, and eventually she was running long runs, which increased weekly until she made it to seventeen miles one Saturday evening.

A couple of times I rode my bike alongside her on these longer runs, which we clocked in at over two hours. I peddled easily along as my daughter pushed herself one step at a time, and in pain most of those steps. Clearly, she was investing a whole lot more than I was during those two hours.

As I accompanied her, I thought about my running days way back when, why I loved running, how I felt like a million bucks after about one and a half miles, and why I eventually quit—I got tired of finding running partners only to have them quit on me a few months later.

So watching my daughter set a goal of running 26.2 miles in one run was amazing to me. Inside, I was cheering her on through every single run she went on.

She endured rain, wind, heat, humidity, potholes, hills and valleys, exhaustion, sickness, and pain, pain, and more pain—knee injuries stopped her in her tracks for over a month.

When it looked like she was finally able to resume running, another obstacle hit hard. A friend died. The decision to run or not was no longer, "Will my body be able to handle running this distance?" It defaulted to a more important choice, sacrificing her hard-earned goal in favor of staying put and supporting her friend's family.

I was never so proud of my daughter than when she told me it wasn't even a hard decision to make. She knew she had to set aside her own dream for the sake of supporting someone she loved. I don't think she realized it, but she had already won her race without even stepping foot on the Chicago race line. To my mind, she chose the best road to travel by stepping up to the moment and choosing to walk alongside her friend's family during a time of great sorrow for them.

She sacrificed every day for months to reach a dream she eventually decided wasn't as valuable as being there for someone who needed her. Her dream might not have worked out as she'd sacrificed and hoped for, but I believe God worked through her to fulfill an even greater accomplishment as she submitted her plans to his bigger one. He always does.

* * *

Ever heard that old song with the catchy lyric, "Dream a little dream with me?" I wonder a lot about making grand plans, pursuing bold dreams, and going after what God has placed upon my heart to accomplish. I believe hope and dreams are the stuff of life. God created us to create. The more we use those gifts, the happier we are because in those lovely creative moments, we resemble our creator. And I believe God smiles down on us.

Which begs me to consider what God desires of us when, in the madcap pursuit of those same dreams, obstacles enter our lives that force to us to choose between them. Stop signs halt us from every direction, and we're left with a job unfinished, a goal unreached, or a heart undone and broken with sadness. It seems to me that God wants us to exhibit the same zeal we put toward reaching our dreams into relinquishing of them. The more I recognize God's absolute right to ownership over me and my dreams, the more comfort I draw knowing he orders my days for his glory and my very best.

Some Christians are known for saying, sometimes rather glibly I might add, the phrase, "Lord willing." While I agree with that statement one-hundred percent, I have to ask myself how often I pray the prayer that never fails, "Thy will be done on earth as it is in heaven," and really mean it? Because if I truly believe that statement then I'm saying God knows more than I do about the path I should take and he has the right to move me into a different direction, even if it's mere seconds before I see my dream come to fruition. This willing submission is at the heart of my love for God. His will. His way. Always the right way.

Takeaway Thought: The sooner I accept your divine plan, interruptions and all, over my own, the quicker my heart begins to heal and I start to see the beauty of your bigger story.

I lift my burden to you, Lord,

There's so much I don't understand about making plans and working toward our dreams. This is especially true when I truly believe You've led me toward a specific goal and then some detour enters my life and I have to abandon it. Help me to never waiver in my trust in your divine plan for my life. The more I submit my hours and days to you, the smoother the road becomes because I'm working in partnership with you. Thank you for caring about the even the smallest details of my life. Amen.

Chapter Fourteen
Doubt: When Lack of Trust Protects Us

Teach me knowledge and good judgment.
—Psalm 119:66

Is it possible that doubt might be one of those unwelcome guests of life that is sometimes, in the right circumstances, good for you?
—John Ortberg

Some years back I experienced one of those "I never saw it coming scenarios," when I felt betrayed (and played) by someone pretending to be my friend. Looking back, I should have seen it coming, but I wanted to believe that this person would never do to me what I'd observed her doing to others. As naïve as it sounds, I honestly thought that if I was straightforward, honest, and treated this person with kindness and respect, I would be protected from any relational fallout. I was wrong.

The curious thing about this troubling situation was that I had inklings of this individual's unhealthy pattern in relating to people. I watched her blow up and then verbally incinerate those who angered her. I heard her speak with spite and jealousy against those she didn't like. I listened to her complain about how no one appreciated her efforts at work. Perhaps most telling were the words she used to describe herself and her dealings with others. Made me shudder and give thanks that I wasn't her enemy.

Still, I kept believing that as long as I did the right thing, said the right thing, and treated her well, our friendship would never have to go down one of those awful detours that destroy friendships. In short, my illusions were short-lived and the saddest part of this story is that I never did figure out what I did to anger my friend. But the inevitable happened, the friendship just faded away and no amount of apologizing or trying to work through the issue ever helped.

Once I finally realized I was just one more "friend" in a long line of people this happened to, I felt angry (at myself for not seeing what was obvious) and I felt deeply hurt (because I had really cared about this person.) The farther I moved away from the emotion of the fallout, the more clearly I could look back and see that the signs had been there all along. Still, it stung.

After several years passed by, I gained even more clarity and realized that every step of the way, God was trying to warn me (and temper my expectations), but I chose to ignore the obvious. That's when I learned an important lesson: there's an upside to doubt. God wants us to be as wise as serpents but as innocent as doves. In other words, not everyone who wants to befriend us has our best interests at heart. Doubt in the right circumstances is a good thing.

* * *

Author Paul Tripp wrote something about relationships many years ago that has always stuck with me. He said this, "If you're dealing with an angry person, be assured they will at some time get angry at you. If you're dealing with a distrustful person, be assured they will at some time distrust you. If you're dealing with a jealous person, be assured they will at some time become jealous of you." Tripp is right.

When those around us struggle in specific core ways with anger, trust, jealousy and the like, their weaknesses will eventually spill over into the relationship with us. We all want to believe that our friendship is so special, so treasured, so untouchable, that the patterns by which our friends govern their lives won't come into play with us. Wrong. Wrong. Wrong.

None of us is immune to sin and its side effects that wriggle their way into the heart of all relationships. Which is why listening to God's still small voice of caution is always wise, as is taking note of how others treat the people in their lives. How our friends (new or long-standing ones) treat their closest friends and family members is how they will eventually treat us. Depending upon the friend, that can be a mighty sobering thought.

There is an upside to doubt when it protects us from those who want to harm us. No wonder so much is written throughout the book of Proverbs about entering into relationships carefully and with great prudence. The truth is we do become those we choose to surround ourselves with—for good, for bad, forever.

Takeaway Thought: I become most like those closest to me so I must ask myself if I like what I see. Does God agree?

I lift my burden to you, Lord,

Help me Lord, to let go of friendships that do not honor you. Please give me your sensitivity and wisdom before I start new friendships. Help me to listen to your Spirit's nudges of warning in my heart when entering a friendship that is harmful. I want to believe the best about people, but the truth is, some folks mean me harm. I need your warning system to go off loud and clear in my head and heart so I can avoid needless heartache. All that I have is yours, including every one of my relationships. Guard and protect them, please. Amen.

Chapter Fifteen
Failure: It's Not About Success

I cry out to God Most High, to God, who
fulfills his purpose for me.

—Psalm 57:2

Wisdom is found along a path that is strewn
with our own sets of fears and insecurities to
be faced. We must do the thing we think we
cannot do. It's in the doing that the strength
comes.

—Paula Rinehart

Earlier this week I saw my dentist and, during the
examination, he pressed his thumb into the side of
my neck. Hard. Feel that? Ahhh . . . yes. That's the
"little ball of hate," and you have to work at diffusing
it. He continued, "every day work your hands over
this nerve and try to knead out this area and your jaw
will feel much better. Promise."

Working my neck muscles and wearing my bite
guard 24/7 appears to be a simple fix. Sounds easy,
right? Believe me it's not.

Though I'm complying with wearing the bite
guard all day, every day, and through the night, I'm
finding it much more difficult to locate that "little ball
of hate" in my neck. I work my fingers all over my

neck muscles but I can't seem to find the trigger point that my dentist had no problem locating.

Hmmm . . . reminds me of the trouble I sometimes have trying to locate, and diffuse, what's really bothering me on the inside of my heart and mind. Deep inside, I frequently have this "little ball of hate" swirling around and it's set off by:

nasty politics, irresponsible journalism, **the** exploitation of women and children, media sensationalism, to name just a few.

In the same way I fumble around looking for the exact nerve that's causing me physical pain, I struggle to find a way to diffuse my inner frustration with the larger ills of the world. I know I can't change everything, maybe not even a few things, but I can do one thing—a single small choice every single day—to make a difference. Which is why I keep writing letters, keep making phone calls, and keep giving to organizations that "fight the good fight." Otherwise, I fail, in my eyes and in God's eyes.

Whenever God calls me to act and I turn the other way, I fail to act as his hands, his feet, and his voice in this broken world. I look at it this way. There are injustices in this world that I hate, hate, hate. But unless I'm willing to step out and speak up, that "little ball of hate" against injustice isn't doing me or anyone else any good. I know the RX isn't sitting around and feeling angry, it's doing something. Anything. Any. Little. Thing. Makes a difference. In the world and inside of me.

The final word isn't whether or not I've fixed the problem. The final word is that I've tried. Fail or not, I've stepped out in faith and made the attempt. Failure is never about success.

* * *

Failure—the word itself conjures up nasty pictures in our mind. We run from failure like we run from the plague. No one wants to fall on their face in humiliation. And yet, if we're honest, everyone grows stronger, fitter, by the mistakes we make. We watch children fall and get back up again. Fall and get back up again. Sometimes, they fall so many times it takes an adult to call it quits for a time of recovery. One of the reasons I don't think small children are much daunted by trying and failing is that their little brains haven't yet connected the cause/effect principle. To kids, risk is still just a word in a dictionary not a painful memory.

For adults, we're just the opposite as we've experienced far too many moments when embarrassment stole our peace in the most awkward and hurtful settings. Stinging memories of having been shamed or shutdown by those we care about (or whose opinions we value) hinder us from risking failure today. Even when the cause is important, too many of us pull back in hesitation when God says move into the fray. Shame on us.

Since most of life entails risk, why not step out in faith on behalf of those who have no voice? Why not move into a tricky situation with the strength God provides and watch him work wonders? Why not offer our gifts and talents to those who might reject our kindness? Why not? Success or failure is never the issue. It's all about obedience even when we're risking that which we most value.

Takeaway Thought: Whether I succeed or not is never the point, it's whether I act on what I know to be the right course of action.

I lift my burden to you, Lord,

I'm a coward and so prone to being a people-pleaser that I'm often afraid of speaking out boldly against the evils I see around me. I'm ashamed that I frequently care more about guarding my reputation than stepping out in faith for the well being of others. Help me to move into any arena, at any time, anywhere I'm needed, knowing that if you call me, you'll also supply everything I need when I get there. Amen.

Chapter Sixteen
Workplace: Where Gifts and Talents Shine Bright

It is God who arms me with strength and
makes my way perfect.

—Psalm 18: 32

Sometimes we need guidance over tough
terrain, and other times all we really need is
some company.

—Vinita Hampton Wright

It's been said that up to 80 percent of working men
and women hate their jobs. I believe it. From where I
sit, this statistic is one of the saddest commentaries in
life. To think that the setting where most people
spend the bulk of their hours and days is a place they
despise is, well, unthinkable. But it's oh so common.

Reflecting back in my own life to my early
twenties, I remember lamenting daily to my
longsuffering mother, think about that word
longsuffering, about how I felt impatient and so full of
angst to find the right vocational fit for myself. I tried
retail, restaurants, accounting—nothing made my
heart sing. In all honesty, it wasn't until I had given
birth to my eldest daughter and was a stay-at-home-
mom that I discovered my love for writing. That's
when the vocational clicking happened to me. Looking

back, I can see how God open and closed doors for me along the way, and I was finding out a lot about my strengths and weaknesses every step of the way.

Still, I recall keenly the emotional distress I felt at that young age, and I remember praying that God would help me figure out what he wanted me to do given how he created me. Eventually, he answered that prayer. But it wasn't until I'd experienced lots of bumps and bruises and even more vocational mishaps, mistakes, and setbacks during those early years. Of course, I now understand that God was wanting me first to trust him and to submit myself to his timing and plans for me. But it was hard. *Longsuffering* comes to mind as I then believed that particular season of waiting would never come to an end.

The fact is, and always will be, God is always more interested in making me more like Jesus than he is with my shortsighted pleading prayers to make my life one big happy, happy, happy adventure. And I realize something now, I wouldn't be able to accomplish the work God has given me today if I hadn't endured those rough patches through the years. Our experiences give us the opportunity and the voice to speak into others' lives with a keen effectiveness that comes only after we've dug some trenches and emptied stinky garbage cans with our blood, sweat, and tears. Only then can God use our gifts and talents to shine bright in the workplace because character always comes first.

* * *

Author Jerry Bridges writes in his excellent book, *Trusting God*, that so many folks are unhappy in their workplaces primarily because they use the wrong tools to select their career. Bridges believes that the majority of people struggle against who God made them to be, and rather than trying to discover their talents, gifts, and natural bents, they rail against their God-given design and choose careers where they won't succeed.

Makes sense to me. I would guess that we've all observed men and women who pursued certain career paths because they blindly followed in their parents' footsteps. Others chose their colleges and subsequent careers because they felt pressured by peers to do so. Still more select vocations solely based on the how much monetary return they'll receive. None of these reasons alone are good parameters for making career choices.

I've always been a fan of those gifts and talents testing services where individuals can fill out the forms to find out what types of workplace scenarios they'll be most likely to succeed at and be happy doing. Another good way to discern what areas might be worth pursuing is to listen to others' assessments of what you excel at—we often don't see ourselves clearly, but onlookers do. When a person consistently hears others telling her she excels at leading, take note. When someone tells me I've encouraged them, I take note. When I observe an individual handling money expertly and I tell them so, they take note. There are clues all around us that God uses to direct our paths, and some of those can be unveiled through the comments and observations of people we trust most.

Another key principle to workplace success is embracing the truth that God uses even the most unlikely work situations and people to bring out our best (and worst) so that we grow strong in character. If you have a wonderful boss, thank God for him. If you are dealing with an unreasonable boss, then thank God for the opportunity to show unconditional love toward that person and perhaps be used as the instrument to bring that difficult one to saving faith in Christ. That scenario happens every day— a strong-hearted, hardworking employee who submits first to God and then to his unreasonable employer— what better way to shine bright?

Takeaway Thought: No matter where I work, no matter who I work for, no matter what I do, I ultimately work for you, God.

I lift my burden to you, Lord,

It's been a long haul trying to figure out what type of work is best suited for my specific gifts and talents. Help me to be wise as I make vocational decisions, since they affect such a large portion of my life. Give me your perfect perspective and enable me to wait with good grace if I'm in a job that I don't really like. I comfort myself with the truth that you have all my days charted before the beginning of time and that you created me to fulfill your good purpose in this world. Thank you for your guidance, your goodness, and your perfect provision. Amen.

Chapter Seventeen
Care Giving: Sacrificing for Another's Comfort

Surely God is my help; the Lord is the one who sustains me.

—Psalm 54:4

Accepting the help of others is one of the best and most difficult ways of fostering loving relationships.

—Gary Chapman

Some years ago I answered the phone only to hear my almost always emotionally level friend—a trait I was somewhat envious of through the years—dissolving in tears at the other end of the telephone line. Picture this scenario: My single mom friend with her three teens is asked by her elderly parents to sell her home, help them (the elderly parents) sell their house, and jointly move into a different house accommodating both families so that my friend can help care for her parents as they age. My friend, being the selfless, godly woman that she is, sells her home and moves into the new house. Within a few days of that move, my friend's mother calls and tells her they (the elderly parents) have changed their minds about moving.

Who can picture living through this living nightmare? My friend could and she did. Sadly, it wasn't just a bad dream that she could sit up in bed and shake off, it was her reality. After countless conversations and pleadings by her folks to agree to the joint household living situation, my friend agreed. Who could have predicted that her parents would abruptly change their minds, leaving my friend in a lurch financially and emotionally bereft? No one.

What transpired on the heels of that phone conversation was the very last thing my friend could have imagined and to say that her parents' decision to not move strained their relationship would be an understatement. Still, my friend "manned up" and made the best of this awful situation, which was further complicated by the ongoing fact that her parents still needed care giving. In the ensuing months, my friend and her children's lives eventually returned to some normalcy. However, my friend was abruptly thrust into a new dimension of care giving she hadn't counted on or expected.

After that significant and taxing event, she started making ground rules with her folks that she hadn't previously realized were needed. She also took a few steps back and began re-assessing her parents' needs as well as her own. Some of the choices she made angered her parents. Others, they only bristled at but later complied when they realized it was for their protection. To say that my friend learned a few lessons about the role of care giving would be accurate, and what she discovered was that even when you're fully prepared, you're not fully prepared. Making sacrifices so that someone you love is comfortable, sometimes remarkably so—that is care giving in a nutshell.

* * *

Care giving is one of the most noble and selfless acts of service we can offer those we love. Whether it's short-term care giving following an accident or illness or the long-term variety that comes with aging, taking care of people is a beautiful loving act. But as is true in every area of life, care giving will throw us some curveballs, so preparation is non-negotiable.

What may begin as a short stint in giving some additional care can swiftly morph into a 24/7 responsibility. Which is why looking ahead just makes good sense as we anticipate various solutions to impending problems. Depending upon a number of factors, families can somewhat accurately predict what their loved one is going to face and how they might best meet those needs. We look ahead and then we assess our resources (people, time, money) and start the delegation process. Above all, we bathe the situation in continual prayer asking God to reign over the whole situation.

Like so many service-oriented endeavors, care giving has its high points and low points. There will be an ebb and flow to the entire process, one that can be tempered by realistic expectations of everyone involved. It's never easy being the person on the receiving end of care giving. It's never easy being the person giving the care. It is, however, something we do for those we love and we try to do it with a generous and kind spirit.

The fact is, this care giving cycle never really begins or ends. It is how God created humankind to function best. I need you today. Tomorrow you may need me. Give. Take. Bless. Receive. That's the kind of circle of life we can be glad to be a part of whether we're 8, 18, 48, or 98. Care giving is simply ageless.

Takeaway Thought: Planning, preparation, delegation, and prayer are the tools I require to be an effective caregiver.

I lift my burden to you, Lord,

Nothing would please me more than to have the opportunity to take care of those I love when they are sick or as they age. And yet, I know that in my own strength all my good intentions will not be enough. I need your guidance, your wisdom, your enablement to tackle this challenging service to others. Help me to plan wisely, prepare as much as I am able, delegate whenever I can, and pray, pray, pray all along the way. Thank you, Lord, for giving me both the desire and the ability to serve in this way. Amen.

Chapter Eighteen
Parenting: Speaking up to Influence a Life

How sweet are your words to my taste,
sweeter than honey to my mouth!
—Psalm 119: 103

Talk is not cheap because interpretation is not
cheap. The way we interpret life determines
how we will respond to it.
—Paul David Tripp

Sometimes specific conversations stick in our minds
because of the emotion they evoked. Other times, we
remember someone's words because they were able
to state what we have been feeling but unable to
articulate. One of the most memorable
conversations that will bubble to the surface of my
mind whenever I face a parenting challenge (or
heartbreak) is a simple observation my closest
friend spoke.

We were discussing our current parenting roles
and responsibilities and how they were changing yet
again as our post-high school children were now
college students, college graduates, new to the
workforce employees, some still single, and some
married with kids. In short, our kids were now
grownups. What my friend said to me was this,

"Whoever said that parenting ends when your children turn eighteen was wrong. Dead wrong." Agreed.

Not to discourage any young moms and dads out there, but look at parenting through this little equation: little people = little problems, big people = big problems. When our kids were small, we attended to their scraped knees, splinters, and playground fights. As our children grew to adulthood, so did the magnitude of their problems in life. Instead of scraped knees and childish spats, our kids are now facing, well, the very same problems we parents face. Relationships that sour. Jobs that are lost. Finances that don't quite cover expenses. Burdensome educational loans. Pricey car repairs. Unending home maintenance. Life ravaging illness and disease. Tricky childrearing issues of their own.

Never in my younger parenting years could I have imagined the mental strain and emotional pain I've endured since my four children have graduated from high school. Much of the time, I was just praying to get them graduated from high school. Silly me. How was I to know that the parenting journey (like most of life) would become steeper and demand far more of me spiritually, mentally, emotionally, even physically, than in the earlier years?

I don't suppose we should spread this fact around to the young moms and dads out there, lest they shrink back from parenting altogether. But it's true nonetheless. As your kids age, you'll be forced to face one season of letting go after another, as well as being forced to accept that parents of young adults have precious little control over their children's lives. We know and accept intellectually that we have no control, but our emotions struggle to keep pace with this ever-morphing role of parenting.

There is, however, one area where God gives moms and dads more control with each passing year. It is the weighty burden and privilege to intercede like never before. Parents now, finally, have the insight of age, experience, and hopefully lots of wisdom that they can use to fuel their prayer for their kids. Speaking, praying, and exhorting our young adults toward God's best for them becomes the primary mode of operation for parenting well, the kids, who are now adults, whom God has placed under our charge.

* * *

There is a tendency to try and peek around the next corner of life whenever we're in the messy, muddled struggles of parenting young kids. I used to long for the day when all four of my children were out of diapers. Then I longed for the day when they understood what it meant to lay on their beds and stay there for a quiet time. Next, I longed to get to summer when I could get a break from homeschooling. You guessed it, by mid-July, I was longing for the routine of a brand new school year. I was perpetually longing. Silly me.

I've found that I can't really value and appreciate life when I'm always longing for the next season to arrive. One insight I have discovered through lots of trial and error, too much error on my part, is that how I think affects how I feel which affects how I act. Make sense?

When I think in biblical terms, I can put all my hope and trust in God's perfect provision for me and my kids for today (just today), and my mind and emotions reflect that beautiful truth. Which in turn affects the words that come out of my mouth. Pleasant. Patient. Kind. Gentle. Loving. Sounds good to me (and my kids). I've learned to give thanks for this day, this hour, no matter what it brings. I deeply desire to speak words that will encourage and equip my children to face their trials in ways that honor God and that enable them to overcome whatever challenges arise. No matter how old I am, no matter how old my kids are, the ABCs of childrearing always begins and ends with *trust him,* and then say so out loud.

Takeaway Action Thought: What I lose in control over my kids' lives, I can gain in influence by speaking, praying, and exhorting them with my words.

I lift my burden to You Lord,

I never expected parenting young adult children to take so much out of me. There have been times when I wanted nothing more than to turn back the clock so that I could control what they do, where they go, and protect them more. As I age (and my kids age) it becomes more and more apparent that how I think, how I speak, makes all the difference in my attitude and outlook. Help me Lord to give thanks for every situation knowing that You transform the difficulties into strength to face the future. My kids have been and always will be Yours. Amen.

Chapter Nineteen
Financial Setbacks: Finding
Freedom in Our Material World

Whom have I in heaven but you? And earth
has nothing I desire besides you.

—Psalm 73: 25

We are not just physical stuff; we are spiritual
beings. And our deepest hunger is spiritual.
We hunger for meaning. We hunger for love.
We hunger for redemption.

—John Ortberg

Money. Money. Money. We can't live without it,
and most of us don't know how to live with it
successfully. Let me rephrase. Most of us don't know
how to live lives not confined by money, and what it
can buy. I've seen this operate over and over again in
my own life. Ever since I took my first job as tomato
picker when I was at the tender age of fourteen, I've
been trying to make my little stretch into a lot. I
would play around with the figures in an attempt to
save more, spend less, and still have enough for my
needs.

I played this numbers game time and again into
my early twenties, until I said, "I do," almost twenty-
nine years ago and handed the budgeting plan over to
my thrifty spouse. While we've always been frugal,

there have been a smattering of times when we had extra money and we happily splurged. But for the most part, we routinely checked our online budgeted accounts before taking off with the credit cards or cash and spending. All this is the backdrop to my current financial state of mind.

The last few months have been awful. My husband and I decided I needed to work off a cash system because I kept spending next week's budgeted amount this week. Now, we're not talking about thousands or even hundreds of dollars overspent. It was more in the forty and fifty dollar range, but even those miniscule amounts signaled something was off kilter in my thinking. I was continually playing a mind game of, "I can buy what I want today because I'll have the money before the bill arrives." True confessions hurt, don't they?

Because the monetary value was small, I excused myself and my faulty thinking. Finally, my loving spouse challenged me with the principle of the thing, and a lesson we consistently taught our four kids. You don't buy if you don't have the cash today to back it up. Ouch. Point taken.

The painful part was putting this discipline back into practice. But as I started re-evaluating all my purchases, including my needs, wants, and impulsive buys, I realized God was helping me develop a deeper contentment on the inside. I was also much more aware of how much the media still influenced what I bought and why. Going to the cash-only system has sparked a new level of sensitivity—and dare I say freedom?—in the way I'm spending and living. God's Word tells us to pay attention to the details in life because they can alter our entire life's path. Financial freedom starts with saying no when we need to, or even when we don't.

* * *

One of the most valuable spiritual and financial lessons we can learn is that all the material goods in the world won't satisfy us for long. Don't believe me? Try reading the book of Ecclesiastes nice and slow. You'll see that even Solomon in all his glory and wealth beyond measure wasn't content with his hoard of stuff. Solomon went even further to try and fill his heart's needs by buying, building, or burying himself in one extravagance after another. Nothing. Nothing. Nothing. Absolutely nothing satisfied.

Ever wonder why God included the specific true stories throughout the bible that he did? It's our roadmap for our lives, that's why. We can learn from our forefathers' mistakes and errors, and if we're smart, avoid them. I've often read and reread the book Solomon wrote and thought to myself, "If the wisest man who ever lived tried everything under the sun and he wasn't happy, then I should save myself the trouble, the grief, and the expense." Still, human nature being what it is, we have our moments when we mentally wander and wonder what it would be like.

All in all, I'm grateful for the financial parameters God has placed around my life. There have been countless key decision-making junctures when either the surplus or lack of money helped to guide us where God intended wanted us to go. Since he owns everything on earth anyway, we should trust him enough to know how much money we can handle without becoming independent of him and turning to our own ways and wisdom. Money. Money. Money. We can't live without it and most of us don't know how to live with it successfully until we turn to and take heed of God's unfailing Word on the matter.

Takeaway Thought: Above all, I am a spiritual being, and when my spiritual self is focused aright, everything else in the material world falls into its rightful position.

I lift my burden to you, Lord,
    I wonder how many times I've used material things to soothe a wounded heart? How often have I spent money needlessly, carelessly, just because I didn't feel good on a particular day? Lord, help me first to recognize that every single thing I own is yours and you expect me to be a wise steward of these resources. Next, please help me to develop a thankful and contented heart so that I'm never trying to fill my heart with stuff that doesn't satisfy. Only you, Lord, only you, can fill and satisfy the longing inside of me. Amen.

Chapter Twenty
Relocation: Downsizing to Upgrade for Better Quality of Life

I will instruct you and teach you in the way
you should go; I will counsel you and watch
over you.

—Psalm 32:8

Life always plays in a forward direction; it
never goes backward. Once a move is made,
there is no going back.

—John Ortberg

I once read that as we age there will come a time
when we have nothing left but Jesus. As I get older, I
can attest to the fact that we continually have to
relinquish control over more and more of what we
value most. Physical strength. Mental sharpness.
Friends and loved ones who get sick or pass away.
Vocations that we are no longer competent to handle.
The list can go on and on and on. Relinquishment
and aging go hand in hand.

Another saying I've never been able to shake, nor
do I want to, is "If you can't get over, under, or
around a particular obstacle"—like aging for
example—"you might as well negotiate with it."
Excellent advice. In order to let go with good grace,
I'm learning to hold everything with a looser hand. I

recognize that today's good health, mental awareness, treasured relationships, and workplace opportunities are going to end at some point, which is why I'm trying to look ahead into the distant future and give God the okay to relocate me if needed. Can you hear God chuckle?

Relocate. The very word can summon up negatives images of boxes, moving vans, and for sale signs. But it doesn't have to be so. Relocate can be revamped into something far more positive and promising. I've known folks who have to relocate every few years and love it. Though the concept is foreign to me, I want to emulate their spirit of adventure. New people. New experiences. New sights, smells, tastes, and sounds. New can be a very good thing.

Relocating doesn't have to mean downsizing and giving up what matters to us, rather relocation can enhance our quality of life. We aren't necessarily taking a step backwards; we are proactively stepping into a future more suited to our changing life and lifestyle. Life is always in motion. So why not begin adapting our thoughts to the possibility of relocating when the time is right?

* * *

Precious few individuals begin and end their lives in the same location. Those who do are the exception rather than the rule. Change. Moving. Relocating. Relinquishing. It's all a part of living a full life. None of us can turn back the clock and retreat backwards in time. All of life moves forward. So must we.

Change. Moving. Relocating. Relinquishing. Let's stop the negativity cycle that has laid its grip on our hearts and minds when we consider these parts of life's events. Instead, let's accept the fact that God has designed our lives so that we enter this world completely dependent upon the care of others and most often will leave this world in the same way. Let us also seek the eternal perspective that Christ frequently taught throughout Scripture that when a man gives up his life, or control over it, he gains it back big time. In the topsy-turvy spiritual realm, relinquishment is always viewed as a positive, life-giving act of service to him, and the rewards are literally out of this world.

Rather than waste today fretting about what hasn't yet happened, why not learn to increase our trust quotient with Christ's perfect care for today and the unknown tomorrow? Though it's true that with aging comes relinquishment, the fact is, the more we rely on Christ, the more he becomes our everything. I do believe that as we grow older we feel our limitations more keenly. However, what we fail to realize is that with every strength, choice, or option we give up, Christ himself more than makes up for these losses with who he is. Christ becomes our strength. Christ becomes our hope. Christ becomes our heart to heart confidante. Christ becomes our purpose for living. Christ and Christ alone.

Takeaway Thought: Some of the best experiences of my life have begun only after I intentionally decided to relinquish control to you.

I lift my burden to you, Lord,

Change, any change, tends to frighten me, Lord. If I had my way, I would keep everything as it is right now. I realize that is not faith-filled thinking, but frustrating, shortsighted, stuck thinking. Help me to accept every new season in my life with good grace. Remind me that you orchestrate all my hours and days. To the tiniest detail, even where I set my head down at night, you guide and watch over me. Thank you, Lord, for your constant and unwavering care for me. In my heart of hearts, I do trust you, Lord; I'm just so very aware of my increasingly dependent mind, body, and soul. Amen.

Chapter Twenty-One
Divorce: When "I Dos" Don't Last

A father to the fatherless, a defender of
widows, is God in his holy dwelling. God sets
the lonely in families.

—Psalm 68: 5–6

That is what our friendship groups are. They
are our safety nets. Because sometimes you
fall so hard that you need more than one
person to catch you.

—Sarah Zacharias Davis

Before I received that ominous telephone call, I can
tell you plainly that I couldn't have cared less about
the national divorce statistics being in excess of a 50
percent failure rate. All I cared about was that my
best friend feared her marriage was over, and it broke
my heart.

I still remember the evening she called and my
friend began telling me that her then-husband was
making all sorts of complaints about his life, their
marriage, and her specifically. What boggled my
mind was that this behavior was so uncharacteristic
of this particular guy. Always easy-going, seemingly
happy, I would never, ever have predicted the
upcoming heartache that was about to fall on my
friend and her three young children.

Talk about life throwing you a curveball. This turn of events left everyone who knew this couple shocked and scratching their heads trying to make sense of it all. And my dear friend of over forty-five years? Well, we had traversed lots of painful territory together but never anything like the loss of a marriage. In the days that followed that phone call, when I mistakenly told her everything would be okay, I think we talked every night for months. So terrific was the blow of her husband's departure that just getting through the day's responsibilities was utterly overwhelming to her, and her children. Who could think about the distant future when today was too painful to endure?

For both of our sakes we would talk each evening, and then I'd ask her, "So what do you absolutely have to do tomorrow?" She would tell me. Then we'd discuss a workable way to get it done. Over time, the daily phone conversations began to stretch out until we were chatting only a couple of times a week. A curious thing happened during that time, and I don't believe we noticed it until years later.

As my friend's marriage began to die a slow death, our friendship started to flourish. It was also in the midst of this emotionally horrific season that my friend found faith in Christ. We've talked about it numerous times since, how God allowed one type of death (her marriage) but ushered in another kind of new life (eternal life in him). While making a commitment to Christ didn't erase the betrayal or take away the pain, my friend will tell you that Christ walked alongside her and made the journey bearable. Once my friend placed her trust in Jesus, I began to breath a lot easier because I knew one thing for sure and certain, he would never let her fall too far.

* * *

During life's most painful intersections when we feel like we are being suffocated by pain, we often discover the power of our friendships to keep us from falling too far. Isn't that what true friendship is really all about? A joining of hands and hearts that won't allow someone we love to fall too far? No matter what the personal cost to us, we secure our friend from giving up, going under, or being trampled over. It's what friends do for each other.

You might need me today. Tomorrow I may need you. It's all about staying close enough to hear a friend's cry for help and then doing something about it. Another thing about friends is the constancy of their loyalty and their willingness to forgive each other when one fails. In little ways or large, real friends understand that we're all going to let one another down eventually. But true friends never let that fact get in the way when their friend is hurting. Just like Jesus said, there is no truer love than to lay down one's life for a friend.

I lay down my life for you by giving you my time, my attention, my listening ear. You love me by forgiving me, speaking truth to me, and guiding me back on track when I stray. We love each other through undying loyalty, unwavering commitment, and unconditional acceptance. Friends don't let friends fall too far.

Takeaway Thought: My friends are my safety nets and my sounding boards in every situation I face.

I lift my burden to you, Lord,

From childhood on, you've blessed me with faithful, loving, and supportive friends. Words cannot express how grateful I am to have people who love me no matter what. Help me to never take these dears ones for granted and show me how to express my love to each of them in ways specifically suited to them personally. Love them, Lord, through my actions and through my prayers for them. Amen.

Chapter Twenty-Two
Retirement: Exchanging One
Vocation for Another

I was young and now I am old, yet I have
never seen the righteous forsaken or their
children begging bread. They are always
generous and lend freely.

—Psalm 37: 25–26

Life is committed relationships of self-giving
love with those whom you would normally
not hang out with: those whom you don't
always like; those who don't share your
zip code.

—Leonard Sweet

Are you thinking of retiring? If you are, please don't. Let me explain. The older I get the more I get that a little more rest, a slower pace, and a more reasonable to-do list is in order. After all, every living thing under the sun is winding down. It just is. So, I really do understand people who dream about retiring from their 9 to 5 jobs in favor of a more relaxing (and perhaps more satisfying) season of life.

What I'm totally opposed to is the idea that once a person retires from their vocation they are devoid of any obligation to continue serving others and adding value to the human race in general. Nada. I'm not quite sure where we Americans have gotten this whole concept of retirement equals entitlement; but I can tell you one thing, it didn't come from the bible I'm reading.

In fact, if you are a bible scholar you already know that Jesus advocates giving our lives away in service to others. He instructs those who follow him to always be looking out for the welfare and needs of people around us. The whole idea that retirement equals entitlement is unbiblical. Clearly so. Certainly, there is a definitive transition between a full-blown career and the more flexible years that follow. Vocation turns into avocation. But the underlying principle of service never goes away.

I recognized this truth most recently when I led a women's class at my church and one of the older ladies (eighty-one years to be exact) began sharing how God was continually bringing younger gals into her life (locally and long distance) to counsel, encourage, and minister to. What struck me most was that this married mom of five adult children and lots of grandchildren continued to love and serve her extended family as she always had done throughout the years, and in addition she continued to serve women outside her family too. Even though her mind and body are slowing down, her spirit is gaining momentum. I marveled at what God could do with a person given over to his purpose no matter what her age. I looked at her and silently thought to myself, I want to be her when I grow up! Then I told her so.

* * *

The word *retirement* conjures up lots of colorful mental images in our aging society. Commercials, magazine articles, and major motion pictures consistently advertise the good life awaiting those who pass the finish line and enter retirement in earnest. But the real truth to fully enjoying those golden years isn't what mainstream media has promised. In fact, it's the polar opposite, and there are studies to prove it.

Those who retire with a plan to continue working in a volunteer capacity fare better and adjust faster to the suddenly subdued pace of retirement than those who abruptly stop working without any preplanning. For those of us who believe that life begins (and ends) at retirement, think again. This next stage of life, which can now be expected to last twenty to thirty years, can only be truly satisfying if we continue to use our God-given gifts, talents, and loads of experience to build into others' lives.

It may not seem glamorous or exciting but it's true nonetheless. Those golden years will only feel as good as gold if we're given over to whatever God's great plan is for us. To be sure, God will want us to take some risks, enter some uncomfortable situations, and keep our eyes peeled for opportunities to love boldly. Then again, maybe retirement is entitlement: it's the privilege we get to serve others with all the time in the world.

Takeaway Thought: Never let me "retire" from serving the people you send into my life, Lord.

I lift my burden to you, Lord,

Help to me gain fresh vision as I age Lord. I want to serve you and those you bring into my life, for my entire life. Give me the wisdom to reject the world's idea of retirement. Reframe my thoughts and expectations of what it means to grow older. Enable me to discern the path you have for me as I age but never, ever, give way to a self-centered, selfish mindset. You set the example for me, Lord, by giving your life for each of us. Let me not waver in doing the same for others. Amen.

Chapter Twenty-Three
Career Choices: It's Never Too Late for Change

But I am trusting in you, O Lord, saying, 'You are my God!' My times are in your hands.
—Psalm 31: 14–15

You cannot self-generate the necessary "heat" of affirmation, encouragement, and support that are gained from true friendship.
—David McKinley

There's a fine woman I know well, and she is struggling deeply. For whatever reason, this multi-talented midlife gal hasn't yet found her niche in the workplace. From where I sit, I can see how smart, gifted, creative, and savvy she is. But she can't see what I see and I think I know why.

Like most of us, my dear friend is paying far too much attention to what she imagines others are saying about her choices. Granted, every choice we make does in some way impact the people around us, so we do need to take care when deciding. Great care. However, what's wrong in this scenario is my friend's focus. She is comparing her vocational journey with others her own age.

Also like most of us, she thinks she knows what others are thinking, but I know these "others" and they aren't thinking anything negative about my friend. On the contrary, because we all know and love her, we all want to help her find the best vocational niche for her sake. We can see what a marvelous person she is, and we simply want her happiness in life to extend into her work world.

I believe this is yet another example of how good friends can help guide us, instruct us, and counsel us through some of life's most challenging decision-making choices. Career choices. Midstream career changes. Those closest to us observe how we handle conflict, problems, and rough territory. They get to watch us fail some, sure, but they also watch us gather the best part of ourselves together and overcome whatever we're facing. They see what we're too close to see clearly. Make sense?

Comparison will rob a person blind and will leave them in a gutter of mucky, hopeless despair. Isn't it time that we ask our nearest and dearest for their thoughts when we're feeling like work has us slammed against a wall with no escape? Everyone needs the perspective of someone (or many someones) who 1) know us well and 2) can offer us godly, biblical counsel. Friends can do that. Best of all, friends will provide affirmation, encouragement, and support that we cannot, under any circumstance, self-generate.

* * *

Psalm 139 is perhaps the strongest argument for trusting God with our lives both personal and professional. Since God created us, formed us, and knows us inside and out, shouldn't we trust that he will also guide us through this life? Absolutely.

Instead, we struggle and worry and fret and fume trying to find our way through many of life's twists and turns. As we go, we forfeit the peace he promises each of us who know him personally. All day and through the night, God assures us he is working on our behalf. Jesus himself is now at the right hand of God interceding for us 24/7.

Still, we refuse his comfort, his guidance, and his messengers (faithful friends and family) who are more than willing to offer a listening ear and words of encouragement. Why? I believe one of the biggest obstacles to discovering God's best vocational fit for us is that we are afraid of what others will think. When an individual takes a position and soon finds out it wasn't what he believed it would be (or that he's unsuited for the job), rather than communicating with his employer (before the boss has spent much time and energy investing in him), he miserably stays put much longer than is wise (or productive).

I'm not one to advocate quitting, anything, but there are circumstances when giving notice is the best choice. Is it humbling? Sure. Is it sort of scary? Yep. Like most of life, you cannot move through the next door until you've walked through the one you're in presently and shut it tight behind you. The book of Ecclesiastes includes a verse about God giving happiness to people through their work. Why not ask God for that special gift right now? Work can equal happiness—it can happen to you.

Takeaway Thought: Keep reminding me to turn to my good friends when I feel confused about life, about work, about everything.

I lift my burden to you, Lord,

Thank you for faithful and wise friends you've placed into my life. I'm always amazed at how much better I feel about life in general and my problems in particular after I've talked with a friend. They help me see the bigger picture. Maybe most important, they remind me to put all my trust in your plan for my life. My friends also strongly remind me how foolish it is to compare my journey with theirs. None of us have it all together; I know this to be true. But sometimes, I also need my friends' words to steer my focus back toward you. Amen.

Chapter Twenty-Four
Physical Illness: When Our Weaknesses Make Us Strong

O Lord, you have searched me and you
know me.

—Psalm 139:1

For all of us, there are inevitable moments
when, even surrounded by loving family and
friends, we feel invisible or go through
something alone. A surgery, a divorce, a
death, a failure. Those sleepless nights, those
closet moments, those tears we shed in
private.

—Carolyn Custis James

There are some things we simply have to endure alone. Physical pain and its accompanying suffering is one of those instances in life that we go through by ourselves. Our families can love and support us, our friends can empathize with us, and our medical doctors can offer us the best care available to modern science, but we alone feel the pain.

This fact was brought home to me each and every time I sat alone in the recovery room after my six shoulder surgeries. My family was waiting for me in the outpatient area; my friends supported me with phone calls, uplifting cards, delicious food, and lots of heartfelt prayer. My doctor and his staff consistently gave me excellent follow up care in the weeks after my surgeries.

Still, I was alone in the recovery process. No one felt the pain but me. No one endured the long weeks of uncomfortable sleepless nights. No one else experienced the sharp knifelike pain that surged through my muscles as I stretched and strengthened my shoulders back into good condition.

These pain-ridden experiences taught me something. There are times and events and sometimes entire seasons when God allows us to be set apart and in pain, so that we learn how very strong he is on our behalf. And, we similarly find out how our very weaknesses can make us strong in him. The spiritual formula I discovered in my moments of greatest weakness is, in Paul's words, "When I am weak then I am strong." It's true.

The more dependent I felt physically, the more I drew my inner strength from the Lord. To be honest, I went through lots of lonely and painful sleepless nights and countless, uncomfortable days when I wanted to give up. And yet God lent his perfect strength and grace to me during those times. He reminded me that I was never really alone. He was upholding me, healing me, protecting me.

Alone we struggle in pain, united to him we prevail over it.

* * *

Down times, as I learned personally, are not wasted times. From our Lord's perspective, I often wonder if he would much rather get our attention in less time consuming, less painful ways. But we're too busy, too driven, too consumed by whatever matters most to us. These varied distractions could even be good things, like family, ministry, volunteerism, friendships, and work.

Often when we're laid out flat on our backs (literally or not), God gets our attention. When he does, we generally listen. Why? Because we don't have any other option. But when God speaks to us during our most painful and weakest moments, the words he has to impart to us can change us forever.

One of the most valuable takeaways the Lord has taught me was during my physically down-for-the-count seasons. I would complain to him that I really couldn't understand why he had me going through the same surgery over and over, the same lengthy recoveries over and over, enduring physical pain before, during, and after each of these episodes. I wanted to serve him. I was eager to get back into service and jump into new areas of ministry.

His reply to my rants? Over and over, I kept sensing (and reading) the same truth I believe God was slowly instilling into my heart. That principle is this: we want to serve from the power position (as Elizabeth Elliot so aptly terms it). We want to give, and serve, and teach, and help others when we are feeling strong, wise, and able. But very often God wants the exact opposite from us. He wants us to serve in those same capacities when we are feeling anything but strong, wise, and able.

Why? His strength is made perfect in our weakness. And, don't miss this truth, God desires for us to be keenly aware that even in our best moments we aren't enough. God wants us to depend upon his enabling every step of the way so that we will know that he did the work. It was him and only him who worked through our weaknesses to accomplish his great good. He loves us. He knows us. The work and the results are his doing. Isn't that enough to know?

Takeaway Thought: When physical pain blinds my way, you are my unfailing support.

I lift my burden to you, Lord,

Thank you Lord for never leaving me alone in my pain. Sometimes, especially when I am alone in the night, I feel abandoned. But your Word tells me that you keep watch over me even in the night hours. Help me to commit more of your promises to memory so that when I'm hurting the most, I can recall your comforting words that you will sustain me always. Amen.

Chapter Twenty-Five
Relational Stress: When Emotions Become Obstacles

O God, do not keep silent; be not quiet, O
God, be not still.

—Psalm 83:1

Feelings, and feelings, and feelings. Let me try
thinking instead.

—C. S. Lewis

Dread. I'm feeling lots of it these days. There's a conversation coming that I'd do just about anything to avoid. Wish I could. Wish I could. Wish I could. But in my heart of hearts, I know I have to summon up some backbone and the courage to open up a topic (again) that's always been a difficult one to address. And because I care about this person deeply and cannot imagine living life without this individual, a two-way conversation has to happen. I so wish it didn't.

The sad thing is, even before I speak the first word, I can almost picture this other person physically tensing up— we've gone down this rocky road before. It's a particularly touchy territory since both of us feel so passionately about the subject. It's far more complicated than either of us believing we are right and the other person is wrong. I'd like to think, in some respects, both of us are right. We just come at the issue from different perspectives.

If only it were an intellectual differing of opinions, the stakes would be so much lower. Instead, emotions run high here, too high, and feelings become so intense that our words tend to become inflamed as well. Once the emotions fire up, all the tried and true facts we've rehearsed ahead of time fly straight out the window. "Feelings. And feelings. And feelings. Let me trying thinking instead," C.S. Lewis wrote. I concur. There's nothing I want more than to work through this sticky situation with gentleness, grace, and a calm composure. In theory, and with God's enabling strength, I know it's possible. I also recognize that I must bathe this conversation deeply in prayer before I can expect any lasting peace to be forged between us.

* * *

Relational stresses are part and parcel of all relationships. They just are. The sooner we accept that fact, the faster we can get on with the work of "working through" misunderstandings, miscommunications, and all the other mishaps that plague us humans as we interact one with another. As we consider the people in our lives, one truth that will help us get along better with other folks is this: relationships are messy. As the title of Paul Tripp's book suggests, "Relationships are a mess worth making."

Whether our personal bent is to run toward (or away from) relational conflict zones, every single individual has to deal with those sticky situations from time to time. When we are forced to face something we might have said (or done) that has offended another person, stepping back for a bit until we can take the emotions out of the situation—or at the least lower them a few levels—is a very good beginning. Imagine the power a quiet heart and mind possesses.

Our blessed emotions can spark in us the passion to right a wrong, enter a dangerous scenario to offer needed protection, and to bring the highest form of encouragement to someone we love. As high as our positive feelings go, our darker emotions can pull us just as low. Which is why we must think through a problem before we enter a conversation. Emotions should inform us, not lead us.

I've always paid attention to Proverb 10:19 that says, "With many words comes many sins" (my own paraphrase). The truth is, I've not always heeded this principle. To my own shame and regret, I've frequently spoken out of turn and then, in turn, had to ask for forgiveness. This is why I now try to temper even my most emotionally distraught moments by imagining myself having to go into relational repair mode after talking out of turn. Not a pretty mental picture. My ability to imagine such dismal scenarios has prevented me from impulsively writing an angry email or spouting off in retaliatory fashion. It has also protected those I say I love from my sinful, undisciplined tendency to allow my emotions to lead me rather inform me. The more I quiet down inside, the better I communicate on the outside. And that's good for everybody.

Takeaway Thought: Quieting my heart and mind in prayer is one of the most effective ways to prepare for a difficult conversation.

I lift my burden to you, Lord,
Running from conflict never solves it. I know this. I am deeply aware that when problems arise, you want me to face them with your good grace. You desire unity among your people. Help me, Lord, to quiet myself before you and take the time to pray earnestly for an open heart and mind before I ever open my mouth to speak. Put a rein over what I say Lord and guide every conversation I have to achieve your good and your glory. Amen.

Chapter Twenty-Six
Aging: There's An Art
to Doing It Well

The Lord gives strength to his people; the
Lord blesses his people with peace.

—Psalm 29: 11

You are capable of taking every situation in
your life and representing it in a way that will
lead to joy or to despair. The interpretation is
in your hands.

—Richard L. Ganz

Some years ago, we were living next door to my
husband's elderly, life-long bachelor second cousin
when he became seriously ill for the first time. Since
he had no spouse, no children, and no family close
enough (or young enough) to help him out, it fell to
our family to assist him. As he battled several types of
cancer, an open-heart surgery, diabetes, Parkinson's
and more, we learned a lot about care giving through
trial and error firsthand. He fought one physical
illness after another for five years before he passed
away following a minor hospital procedure.

A few years later, my husband's dad was
diagnosed with esophageal cancer that he fought for
five months before he did. Since we lived in the same
city as my father in law, I was able to spend

considerable time with him during his various medical appointments and cancer treatments. His fight with cancer was extremely painful, agonizingly so. And yet, I recall the time spent with him as more meaningful and memorable than all the previous years when he was healthy.

The farther I move away from these two experiences of care giving, the more I recognize that how we age (and die) is a personal choice. My father in law never once complained, he was consistently thankful for all the help the family gave him. He accepted his grim diagnosis with a grace that still awes me today. I was blessed by his courageous example and still am.

Contrasting this lovely, yet bittersweet experience with our previous care giving stint, there's no comparison. For sure, we were newbies in the care giving arena and undoubtedly did some things wrong, but it was a daily ordeal for me to offer care to this cousin and neighbor. I've often wondered why I will recall with a slight shudder those five years of giving care to one man and not another? I've come to the conclusion that the person we are when we are young multiplies in spades as we age.

If I'm an angry young and middle-aged person, when I'm old, I'll be an outwardly angry person when I'm aged and the social filters have evaporated. This is a huge caution for all of us. I would never, ever, want to burden my family in any way as I age. But the worst weight I could place upon my kids would be to exhibit attitudes of anger, bitterness, selfishness, pettiness, and the like.

None of us can control exactly how our physical bodies will age over time. We can, however, do quite a lot about developing godly character on the inside that will reveal what we value most on the outside as we get older. Make no mistake, as we age those carefully honed social filters will evaporate, and when they do, who we really are is going to become blaringly obvious to one and all.

* * *

Aging. It truly is that bitter or better proposition. You can view people who have the same situation, identical challenges, similar support systems, and yet they approach their difficulties differently. Rather than it simply being a positive or negative outlook on life, I think it goes much deeper. It's all about interpretation.

Those who age with good grace work hard to maintain a hope-full attitude. Those who age poorly (and by poorly, I mean with a defeatist mentality) give themselves over to a hope-less mindset. It's written all over their faces. If I'm convinced that God has charted out my hours and days, and his word tells me he has, then it's up to me to take God at his word and to bring whatever situation I'm in under an interpretation that will honor him. As I learn to interpret the necessary losses that come with aging in line with eternal promises, aging loses its power to defeat me. Similarly, if I only focus on what I'm no longer able to accomplish, then hopelessness will take over.

No power on earth should extinguish the joy and peace that Jesus has placed into my heart. That "no power" includes aging and its accompanying (often distressing) elements. Instead, I must choose joy apart from circumstances to maintain a peaceful attitude. It's all about how we decide to interpret our situations. Aging, it's an art we need to begin developing while we're still young and able enough to do so.

Takeaway Thought: Physical exercise has temporal, earthly value, but investing in my soul and spirit has timeless, eternal worth.

I lift my burden to you, Lord,

I know I'm not alone in my private concerns about the whole process of aging. It's hard to lose physical health and strength as I get older. More difficult still is the very real possibility of dying from a painful disease. Help me Lord to consistently dismantle my fears and worries through the daily meditation of your word. Remind me as often as need be, that you have charted out all my days. You will never abandon me. Thank you for this precious promise. Amen.

Chapter Twenty-Seven
Childrearing: What Letting Go Looks Like

Spread your protection over them.

—Psalm 5: 11

Absorbing the mess is just part of the process
of getting close.

—Philip Yancey

When I opened the manuscript to begin
reading/reviewing the text before me, I had absolutely
no clue how powerfully the message in this particular
book would affect me, shake me, and stir within me
an overwhelming desire to impart the fear of God
into my then teenage children. The book of which
I'm speaking is Carol Kent's *A New Kind of Normal*,
in which she recounts her family's nightmarish reality
when their son was imprisoned for life for killing his
wife's ex-husband whom they believed was abusing
his stepdaughters.

Throughout this riveting story, Kent describes
how she and her husband rebuilt their faith in the
aftermath of their son's shooting spree. Whether or
not Kent's son was justified in the action he took isn't
the point here. What struck me (and hit home to
many of the Kent's friends and acquaintances) was
that this dynamic Christian couple did everything

right as parents, and yet look what happened to their seemingly ideal family.

Kent writes in her book that one brave soul actually admitted to her that they were afraid that if this unthinkable scenario could happen to the Kent's then it could happen to them as well. As I read this text, I kept asking myself the very same question Kent's friend had posed. If this could happen to them, then why not us? This fine, godly family who sincerely loved their son were now (and still are) facing the hard truth that the only time they will ever see their beloved adult child is during weekly visits at the prison where he is incarcerated.

Since I first read about Kent's story, she has published other titles that continue to chronicle their journey in greater detail, but throughout each retelling Kent reminds parents everywhere that this is their new normal. It's hard. It's brutal. But it's all they have to work with. I've considered that ominous statement more times than I can count. I'm reminded of its truth when I receive an email from a dear friend whose son is divorcing his wife. I can see the pain of this truth written across the face of another friend whose daughter has an incurable disease. New normals can be frightening.

In my own parenting experience, this new normal hits me hard every single time my now adult children face now adult problems of a huge magnitude. I realize with dismay that as much as I long to protect, nurture, and shield my kids from this world's pain, I cannot do so. My life is messy. Their lives are messy.

Together we can face the pain and the heartache, but they are discovering for themselves this new normal. Sometimes, in response to some tragic news, I simply free-fall emotionally until the Lord reaches down and catches me.

I don't expect the ensuing years to get any easier either. But I do pray for the Lord's grace to begin relinquishing control (imaginary though it is) more and more as the days go by. When my kids were little, I dedicated them to him. Now, I'm realizing that God took me at my word, because he's allowing trials my merciful mom's heart could never agree to willingly. Letting go a little more each day, this is my new normal.

* * *

In line with the hard parameters that the Kent family must now live with—this new normal—I believe all moms and dads must reach a point when they intentionally say to themselves, "My parenting role has now changed. Instead of playing the role of an intense helicopter mom, I need to purposefully step back, step aside, and step out of the spotlight of my kids' lives. My earlier, more prominent mom position has to take a backstage place now that my kids are no longer kids." So what does this new normal look like?

It means everything about my parenting takes on a more subtle approach, such as giving advice only when asked, not before. Or holding my tongue even when I believe my child might be making a mistake. And refusing my maternal urges to rush into a situation in order to fix it. I know that it's going to be a difficult, sometimes messy transition into this new normal. I also know that the more I embrace it, the more my kids will thank me later in life.

Takeaway Thought: The more I relinquish my children's welfare into your care and keeping, the more peace I experience as they face the trials of life.

I lift my burden to you, Lord,

My mother's heart will never easily let go of wanting to protect and provide for my children. It doesn't matter how old they are, I want to keep them safe. When they struggle, my faith-guided thoughts remind me that nothing can happen to them unless you allow it. But my emotions scream in opposition of this truth. Help me Lord to let go willingly, gracefully, and in full confidence that you love them far more than I ever am able. Amen.

Chapter Twenty-Eight
Relationships: Blessed Be
the Tie That Binds

Love and faithfulness meet together,
righteousness and peace kiss each other.
                              —Psalm 85: 10

An openness, when fitting, makes us a magnet
for the people around us who are longing for
just one person in their lives to be "real," to
listen to their story without raising an
eyebrow, to let them weep without providing
advice.
                              —Carol Kent

We have family and we have friends. If we're blessed, our family members can also be our friends. More often than not, I hear folks register some measure of dismay when they talk about extended (or not so extended) family members and gatherings. We've all heard the saying, "You can choose your friends but you can't choose your family." Because I believe God has a terrific sense of humor by virtue of some of his natural/animal creations, I also think he enjoys a good belly laugh as he carefully places each of us into our birth families. Then, he laughs even more as we marry into our spouse's family of origin.

Despite what each of us may believe we need in a family, God knows us so well he tailor designs every single individual (Psalm 139) before we are even born. Then he places us into the family especially suited for us. Suited how? Suited for our growth in maturity. The older I get and the more folks tell me the real stories about their childhood home lives, the more I realize how odd and eccentric we all are. And when you combine different personality types and opposite natures, there's going to be turmoil and times when you doubt you're all part of the same gene pool.

And still, God knew what he was doing by creating the family in the first place. You take a dad and a mom and several children—all of whom are highly dependent upon one another socially, physically, emotionally, spiritually, and economically—and you've designed a pretty dynamic unit. Whether it thrives according to God's original intent depends upon the many choices of its members. One abiding fact holds true, severing the family bond is costly for everyone.

While I always want to work hard at creating a home environment where my family feels safe and loved, I also know that during those rocky, tumultuous seasons every family goes through, we will all put down deeper roots than if our family dynamic were clear sailing all the way. The winds of adversity blow fierce on every person, but how blessed is the one who knows that no matter what conflicts have arisen in the past her family members will always have her back. Remember proverb that says, "A brother is born for a time of adversity." Aren't you glad that it's true? I am.

* * *

Friends we can walk away from. Family, not so much. Am I ever thankful for this truth. God really did know best when he created the family unit because he understood our sinful human propensity for running from conflict, for giving up too quickly, for failing to hang in there with people over the long haul. If we had our way, we'd probably be changing (and exchanging) family members as often as we change cell phone plans. One thing is for sure, if extricating ourselves from our family of origin were easy, we'd always be eyeing others for an upgrade over the current model.

While there's nothing more satisfying than enjoying wonderfully in depth, heart to hearts with our best friends, I believe when we experience these same moments with family something supernatural takes place. We get a glimpse of God's love for each of us. The creator of heaven and earth, who loves us beyond measure, also knows our deepest failings, yet he unconditionally offers his love to us. Don't our families offer us a similar type of love? They've grown up with us, fought with us, debated with us, forgiven us, stood behind us, and have been hurt by us. And yet, love us they do. That's the wonder of a family. It's a place where I'm real. You're real. And between us that realness becomes a magnet for good things to unfold.

Takeaway Thought: My family knows me better, loves me more fully, and stands with me no matter what road I take in life.

I lift my burden to you, Lord,
    I find it so ironic how you have placed all these different personalities together into this single identity called a family. If I'm honest, there are times when my family drives me crazy and I want to distance myself from every one of them. But mostly, I'm simply thankful that I'm part of such a lively bunch. Help me to be consistent in my sacrificial love, my intercessory prayer, and in investing myself into my family's lives. I never want to take for granted the love, the safety, and the security of family life. Amen.

Chapter Twenty-Nine
House & Home: What Hospitality Looks Like

The boundary lines have fallen for me in
pleasant places.

—Psalm 16: 6

When we are in deep trouble we long to see
some rescuer appear…Suddenly, decisively,
kindness appears. And it is not the kindness
of soft words or a gentle smile but a strong act
of intervention, a mighty deliverance.

—Mel Lawrenz

I have a friend who takes in strays. I'm talking about
people, not the furry canine variety. Ever since we
first became acquainted over forty years ago, this
female pal of mine has offered her house and home to
any number of folks in need. I used to believe that I
had the gift of hospitality because I truly enjoy
planning a wonderful meal, getting the house ready
for guests, and mentally preparing a special visit for
whomever comes over.

Then one afternoon I thoughtfully started to
contrast how my friend literally opens up her house,
giving up rooms in her home to others, not for hours
but weeks and, when need be, months at a stretch. I
open up my home for a few hours, my friend opens

her home for indefinite time periods. That, my friend, is true hospitality. And for some, my friend's acts of generosity are indeed acts of intervention and a mighty deliverance.

It's enough of a wow factor to be willing to set aside your privacy and personal preferences for visiting family members. It is quite another to offer the same sacrificial love and courtesies to those outside your circle of family or even of friends. To feel that inner nudge to say yes to helping someone, or a family of someone's, get back on their feet emotionally, mentally, spiritually, or financially is a serious business and calling.

Over the years, I've observed my friend clean up, cook, launder, and make room for individuals who weren't always grateful or appreciative of her kindness. A few times these needy souls simply ran out of choices and had no other options or plans. But God had a plan. A marvelous plan that included far more than a place to lay their head down at night and three square meals a day. God has used my friend as one of his instruments to redeem people's very lives. He has used her acts of hospitality as the vehicle to bring renewed healing, trust, forgiveness, and hope into countless people's hearts and minds. I've seen it happen in the most unlikely situations and people.

In fact, my friend's ongoing ministry to people who need somewhere to shelter themselves during life's toughest patches has been the catalyst for me to take more faith-based risks. When I get nervous or apprehensive about jumping into the fray to offer what I can to ease some pain or to meet a real felt need, I remind myself of my friend's courageous choices. Her obedience spurs obedience in me. My hope is that my small acts of obedience will then spark a good work in someone else. And so the cycle continues.

* * *

While conducting frequent radio interviews after the release of one of my books a few years' back, a conversational theme quickly developed between myself and the radio hosts. Since my book dealt with finding value in the hardest events in life, on-air hosts consistently asked me for a few closing remarks to give listeners a positive takeaway.

I always closed with these three directives: Determine to stay tender in a tough world and recognize that it takes far more courage to be sensitive to the plight of others than it does to grow calloused and hardened. Next, get comfortable with being uncomfortable. There are precious few scenarios in this life that we can honestly say make us feel comfortable, so comfort is not a worthy goal in itself. When comfort comes, be grateful for it, but don't go looking for it. Lastly, take the next appropriate step even if you feel afraid. Don't let fear hinder you from moving into a new frontier (or out of a familiar one).

These three mindsets are crucial for today's believer to internalize because we live in a dangerous, uncomfortable, painful world. God forbid that we ever grow weary of doing good when we hold the power to offer help when it comes knocking on our doors. Hospitality is a lot like a hospital…we offer all kinds of healing and hope to all kinds of folks, and our doors should always be open.

Takeaway Thought: It doesn't matter how much I have to share as long as I'm willing to share it with a glad and grateful heart.

I lift my burden to you, Lord,

Help me to always be on the lookout for those whom you send to me. Lord, give me discerning eyes to see needs that I can meet and give me the courage to step forward to do so. Everything I own is yours Lord, give me the wisdom and the creativity I require to share, stretch, and season what I possess with a generous spirit. Hone in me the desire to open my heart and my home as you lead. Amen.

Chapter Thirty
Time: Living in This Moment

Trust God at all times.

—Psalm 62: 8

I have little hope for a future brought about
only or primarily by human endeavors and
initiatives. I have great hope for a future
brought about by a God who pulls us forward
by surprises and spurts, ambushing us with
so-beautifuls and blessing the best of our
worst.

—Leonard Sweet

I received word that someone I love dearly is facing
yet another catastrophic event in her life. She
doesn't need this, I think to myself. Already she's
facing down her own father's terminal illness, a
daughter's looming divorce, and the possibility of
losing her job within the next few months. As a
single mom, she's barely making ends meet as it is,
but if she loses her position, well, I don't want to
think about how much harder it will be than it
already is. Sadness. There's a steady stream of ill
tidings and sadness surrounding my dear friend, and
I'm thinking about her all the time.

Utter and complete sadness—for my friend's
plight and for the world at large. That's been the

emotional flavor of the day lately. At times likes these, I have moments when I consider the hardships my loved ones are enduring and it feels like too much. One difficulty piled on top of another. Too much to handle one at a time, let alone all at the same time. In my grimmest moments, I tell the Lord that this would be a great day for him to come back for us. And I mean it with all my heart. It's time, Lord. It's time!

I know my friend feels the burdens are heavier now than at any other time in her life. She's told me so. During our many discussions about how life's challenges seem to hit all at once, we also agreed that God seems to let it rip for a season and then we get a season of reprieve. I think my friend is right. Because God knows our weak frame, he does give us time to rest, regroup, and recharge. Then, undoubtedly, more trials come knocking, and we're forced to go into heavy-duty trust mode again as we work through the hardships. One step forward, two steps back. Making a little progress one day at a time. Time after time.

Rather than viewing life as either difficult or easy, I'd much rather look at the seasons of life as just that, seasons. Small pockets of twenty-four hour segments where God is developing us into what he wants us to be. Why these twenty-four hour segments? God knows we can only handle life one day at a time. Thus, he sets forth life in day-by-day allotments allowing for eight hours of sleep at night. When I face my hardships one day at a time, I know

I can (with God's enabling grace) handle them. My friend concurs. No matter what tomorrow holds, God has promised to provide for our every need. Today, it's all the time we've got. It's all the time we'll ever need.

* * *

In Ecclesiastes 3: 1–8, we read that there is a time for everything under the sun. For some reason, this whole passage brings me great comfort. As I reflect upon the meaning here, I see a pattern and rhythm forming. Seasons flow into and out of one another. When you look at life, you see how true this is and how every living person must cope with its implications.

We can either go with the flow or go kicking and screaming against the tide we're mired in today. Whether or not God has us planting or uprooting, tearing down or building up, mourning or dancing, searching or giving up, speaking or being silent, embracing or refraining, God alone rules this moment, this time, all time, for all time. What we resist and resent most today can sometimes be transformed into the loveliest of surprises tomorrow. We have to remember that the end of the story isn't simply surviving today's battle. It's often how the writer of Ecclesiastes describes what God does when we least expect it, "He has made everything beautiful in its time." Don't you love it? God himself putting his healing hand on what hurts us most, transforming them into something beautiful. If we're paying attention, we'll find him faithful time and time again.

Takeaway Thought: The more I determine to live in twenty-four hour segments as Christ commanded, the lighter my burdens feel.

I lift my burden to you, Lord,

You have promised to never, ever leave or forsake me. I am counting on this promise Lord, because so many times I feel as though my strength is giving out and I don't have the energy to move another step. Remind me to discipline my thoughts to this day alone. The more I take every worrisome thought captive, the less I have to fret about. I know you will never give me more than I can handle. My times are indeed in your faithful hands. For that assurance alone, I can lay my head down at night and sleep in peace. Amen.

Sources – Burden Lifters

1. Ken Gire, The *North Face* of God (Wheaton, Ill.: Tyndale, 2005), 120.

2. Thomas Secker – general quote found online, no book source cited.

3. Max Lucado – general quote found online, no book source cited.

4. Carolyn Custis James, *When Life and Beliefs Collide* (Grand Rapids, Mich: Zondervan, 2001), 56.

5. Edward Welch, Depression, *A Stubborn Darkness* (Winston Salem, N.C.: Punch, 2004), 142.

6. Paul Rinehart, *Better Than My Dreams* (Nashville: Nelson, 2007), 93.

7. Gregory Floyd, *A Grief Unveiled* (Brewster, Mass.: Paraclete, 1999), 28.

8. Jerry Bridges, *Trusting God* (Colorado Springs, Colo.: NavPress, 1988), 102.

9. Carolyn Custis James, *The Gospel of Ruth* (Grand Rapids, Mich.: Zondervan, 2008), 115.

10. Will Samson, *Enough* (Colorado Springs, Colo.: David C. Cook, 2009), 101.

11. Lauren Winner, *Mudhouse Sabbath* (Brewster, Mass.: Paraclete, 2003), 112.

12. Paula Rinehart, *Strong Women, Soft Hearts* (Nashville: Nelson, 2001), 79.

13. Nancy Guthrie, *Holding On to Hope* (Wheaton, Ill.: Tyndale, 2002), 10.

14. John Ortberg, *Faith & Doubt* (Grand Rapids, Mich.: Zondervan, 2008), 11.

15. Paula Rinehart, *Strong Women*, Soft Hearts (Nashville: Nelson, 2001), 167.

16. Vinita Hampton Wright, *The Soul Tells a Story* (Downer's Grove, Ill.: InterVarsity Press, 2005), 152.

17. Gary Chapman, *Love As a Way of Life* (Colorado Springs, Colo.: WaterBrook, 2008), 122.

18. Paul David Tripp, *War of Words* (Phillipsburg, N.J.: P & R, 2000), 15.

19. John Ortberg, *When the Game Is Over: It All Goes Back in the Box* (Grand Rapids, Mich.: Zondervan, 2007), 196.

20. John Ortberg, *When the Game Is Over: It All Goes Back in the Box* (Grand Rapids, Mich.: Zondervan, 2007), 97.

21. Sarah Zacharias Davis, *The Friends We Keep* (Colorado Springs, Colo.: WaterBrook, 2009), 67.

22. Leonard Sweet, So *Beautiful* (Colorado Springs, Colo.: David C. Cook, 2009), 248, 249.

23. David McKinely, *The Search for Satisfaction* (Nashville: W Publishing Group, 2006), 67.

24. Carolyn Custis James, *Lost Women of the Bible* (Grand Rapids, Mich.: Zondervan, 2005), 98.

25. C.S. Lewis, *A Grief Observed* (San Francisco: HarperSanFrancisco, 1961), 452.

26. Richard L. Ganz, *The Secret of Self-Control* (Wheaton, Ill.: Crossway, 1998), 68.

27. Philip Yancey, *Rumors of Another World* (Grand Rapids, Mich.: Zondervan, 2003), 157.

28. Carol Kent, *A New Kind of Normal* (Nashville: Nelson, 2007), 115.

29. Mel Lawrenz, *Patterns* (Grand Rapids, Mich.: Zondervan, 2003), 68.

30. Leonard Sweet, *So Beautiful* (Colorado Springs, Colo.: David C. Cook, 2009), 50.

Acknowledgements

Sometimes the English language falls short. It just does. Especially right now when my heart is full of thanks, and tears of gratitude threaten to spill over as I consider the goodwill of some pretty amazing people who have made publishing another book possible for me.

Like every other author I know, I recognize (again, with gratitude) that it takes a skillset far beyond my own ability to fashion my words into a book that invites savvy consumers to pick up (or click on) to read. Every single time someone reads my work I feel deeply humbled, because as an author and a book reviewer I know how many excellent resources there are to choose from these days.

But right now, I want to give my thanks to my agent, Les Stobbe, who never wavers in supporting me both personally and professionally. Les, you always have my back, and I'm honored to be part of Mr. Stobbe's Neighborhood. May it increase in strength and number every year.

Receiving a new book contract never loses its thrill. Never. Ever. So my sincerest thanks go to Executive Editor Patton Dodd, who gave my proposal a read and then gave me the good news that I would be joining the fine authors at Bondfire Books. Again, the English language falls far short as I wonder how wonder how many ways I can say thanks to you.

To Marketing Assistant Rachel Mueller, I am loving all your fabulous ideas (so keep them coming!) Whenever I see your name in my inbox, I perk up anticipating the good things that await me. Thank you for lending your expertise to my project and to me.

Finally, I want to say thank you to the entire Bondfire Books editorial, design, and production team for making me one happy, happy, happy author. What else can I say but "Thank you! Thank you! Thank you!"

About the Author

Michele Howe is a reviewer for *Publishers Weekly, FaithfulReader.com, Retailers + Resources, Foreword Magazine, TeenReads.com, and KidReads.com,* among many other national and international publications. She has published over 1600 articles and has been featured on numerous radio shows across the country, speaking on topics such as parenting and women's health issues. Her work has been published in *MORE, FIRST for Women, Good Housekeeping, SheKnows.com, BettyConfidential, HelloWorld, Christianity Today, Discipleship Journal, Midwest Living, Parentlife, Fullfill, Christian Single, Single Parent Family, Focus on the Family, PRISM,* and *Connections.* She also does copywriting and manuscript reviewing for several publishing houses, including New Growth Press. Michele is the author of thirteen books for women.

About Bondfire Books and Patheos Press

Bondfire Books, which operates Patheos Press, is an independent epublisher based in Colorado and New York City. We publish fiction and nonfiction—both originals and backlist titles—by today's top writing talent, from established voices to up-and-comers. Learn more about Bondfire, Patheos Press, and our complete list of titles at www.bondfirebooks.com. Follow us on Twitter @bondfirebooks and find us on Facebook at facebook.com/bondfirebooks.

And if you enjoyed this book, please consider leaving a review — even just a sentence or two. Reader reviews can make a huge difference in the life of a book. You can leave a review now on the next page.